war and film

LOCATIONS

series editors:
STEPHEN BARBER AND BARRY CURTIS

LOCATIONS examines contemporary genres and hybrids in national and international cinema. Each book contains numerous black and white images and a fresh critical exploration of aspects of film's relationship with other media, major themes within film, or different aspects of national film cultures.

on release:

projected cities
STEPHEN BARBER

animals in film
JONATHAN BURT

women, islam and cinema
GÖNÜL DÖNMEZ-COLIN

'injuns!' native americans in the movies
EDWARD BUSCOMBE

war and film

JAMES CHAPMAN

REAKTION BOOKS

For Arthur Marwick

Published by
REAKTION BOOKS LTD
www.reaktionbooks.co.uk

First published 2008
Copyright © James Chapman 2008

Printed and bound in Great Britain
by Cromwell Press, Trowbridge, Wiltshire

British Library Cataloguing in Publication Data:

Chapman, James, 1968–
    War and film. – (Locations)
    1. War films – History and criticism
    I. Title
    791.4'3658

ISBN-13: 978 1 86189 347 5

contents

introduction

If this book were a film, it is the sort that would probably best be described as a 'minor epic': minor in that it is compact in size and short in length, but epic in the sense that it covers a massive subject. A theme as conceptually broad and historically diverse as 'war and film' requires either a very small or a very large book. To elaborate on our filmic metaphor, it is a subject that calls for either the narrative economy of a Budd Boetticher or a Michael Curtiz, or the sprawling canvas of a David Lean or a Sergio Leone. *War and Film* is not and does not aim to be either a comprehensive survey of the field or a definitive history of the representation of war in film. It is written, instead, as an introduction to the subject and as a way of offering a preliminary mapping of a field that has remained relatively unexplored from the perspectives of either film studies or cultural history. It is a map sketched using bold strokes; its contours and shades remain to be filled in. The best way to approach this book is as a set of three thematic essays, each of which offers an exploratory discussion of a broad theme. *War and Film* ranges widely across different national cinemas and conflicts – an approach that inevitably compromises depth of analysis for breadth of coverage, though one that I feel is justified here as an attempt to come to terms with a vast subject in a limited space.

There have, of course, been various studies of the war film as a genre, though even so it is not as well represented in the critical literature of film studies as other genres such as the western, the musical and the horror film. The war film genre tends to be understood as 'films about the waging of war in the twentieth century' in which 'scenes of combat are a requisite ingredient and these scenes are dramatically central'.[1] This definition, which excludes films set during earlier conflicts, such as Roman epics, pre-Revolutionary 'westerns' and Northwest Frontier adventures, immediately suggests that the war film is associated with the historical period of modern, industrialized warfare. In fact, the term 'war film' was first used in the US film industry to describe films about the American Civil War. There is always a certain arbitrariness to the issue of genre definition: thus *The Red Badge of Courage* is often described as a war film, whereas *The Horse Soldiers*, another film with a Civil War background that also reflects on the ethical conduct of war, is generally seen as a western.[2] Rather than become bogged down in tedious debates around genre classification, I have opted for a broad and inclusive, if therefore necessarily imprecise, approach that covers some films that might not commonly be described as war films. If the case studies are dominated by films set during the major conflicts of the twentieth century – the First World War, the Second World War, Korea, Vietnam – this simply reflects the fact that these have been more numerous than films about other wars, though as recent films about the Gulf War (*Three Kings*) and civil wars in Africa (*Black Hawk Down*) attest, other modern conflicts have also begun to provide topical subject matter for the film industry.

Some commentators prefer the term 'combat film' to differentiate the genre from home-front dramas (such as *Since You Went Away* or *Millions Like Us*) or films that examine the effects of war on society and individuals (*The Best Years of Our Lives*, *Born on the Fourth of July*). Jeanine Basinger, for example, sees the Second World War combat film as a distinct genre with its own conventions and iconography.[3] Another frequently used term, though a problematic one, is 'anti-war film', used to describe a critical attitude towards war and its conduct, such as *All Quiet on the Western Front*, *Paths of Glory* and *Apocalypse Now*. John Whiteclay Chambers II, for instance, describes *All Quiet on the Western Front* as 'the classic antiwar film'.[4] The conceptual problem here, of course, is that an anti-war film is not simply the opposite of a war film (*All Quiet on the Western Front* could reasonably be described as both), and that even a film that demonstrates the unpleasant nature of the combat experience remains, essentially, a combat film. In this sense an anti-war film is one defined as much by its ideological and moral orientation as it is by its narrative content.

Where this book differs from previous studies is that it is not about the war film as a genre, though war films of one sort or another inevitably feature prominently throughout. It is, rather, a study of the representation of war in film. Hitherto there has been no thoroughgoing attempt to historicize the various modes through which war (as a subject) rather than wars (as specific historical events) have been represented in film. Historians have focused either on the role of film as an instrument of national propaganda during war or on the filmic representations of particular conflicts, such as the Second World War or Vietnam.[5] The discipline of cultural studies, in contrast, has drawn attention to the theoretical issues arising from the visual representation of war. Paul Virilio, for example, has argued that the conduct of modern technological warfare has become dependent upon cinematic techniques – from aerial balloon photography to infra-red satellite imaging – to the extent that it reached a stage 'where the representation of events outstripped the presentation of facts'.[6] The work of Virilio and other French intellectuals such as Jean Baudrillard provides the theoretical basis for the concept of 'virtual war': that idea that in the modern information age we experience war through visual representation rather than through actuality.[7] At the start of the twenty-first century we have reached a turning point in the representation of conflict, since technological advances in the film industry have made it possible for films such as *Saving Private Ryan*, *Black Hawk Down* and *Brotherhood* to create more realistic representations of the combat environment than ever before – albeit that this realism is achieved entirely through artifice.

The aim of this book, then, is to discuss the filmic representation of war rather than to provide a history of the war film as a genre. For this reason I have ranged beyond the narrow definition of the war film quoted above. A film such as Jean Renoir's *La Grande Illusion*, for example, does not fit a conventional definition of the genre in so far as it contains no actual scenes of combat, but it is nevertheless a statement about war, commenting eloquently on the futility of conflict between nations. I have also included some films set before the twentieth century that would not usually be categorized as war films. The idea that the war film itself is essentially a twentieth-century phenomenon is, in any event, extremely arbitrary, since films set during earlier conflicts such as the American Civil War (*The Birth of a Nation*, *Glory*), Napoleonic Wars (*Waterloo*, *Master and Commander: The Far Side of the World*) or even the Hundred Years War (*Henry V*) are as much about the subject of war as those set during the First or Second World War. *The Birth of a Nation* may be the first anti-war film in that it was made with the declared intention 'that war may be held in abhorrence'. And the dedication of Laurence Olivier's *Henry V* 'to the Commandos and Airborne Troops of Great Britain' clearly aligns the film with the war being fought at the time of its release in 1944.

It seems to me that films about war have generally fallen into one or more categories, and that these categories have, in turn, given rise to lineages, taxonomies or modes that can be mapped across different national cinemas. The book explores three of these lineages, which I have labelled 'Spectacle', 'Tragedy' and 'Adventure'. I should state from the outset that I am making no claim that these are the only three modes of representing war. The best way of understanding these lineages is to regard them not as genres in the conventional sense, with their own particular codes and conventions, but rather as loose, broad and amorphous groupings that encompass different styles and narrative forms, that cross the boundaries of nation and genre and that are continuously evolving and mutating in response to a wide array of historical, cultural and industrial determinants. Some films, as we shall see, can be placed within different lineages: while the opening sequences of *Saving Private Ryan* offer us war as spectacle, for example, the rest of the film follows closely the conventions of the 'men on a mission' narrative that is a recurring trope of the war-as-adventure film.

Each chapter begins with a case study of one film that highlights certain thematic and aesthetic issues relevant to the representation of war and then expands outwards to cover the wider contours of the subject. Chapter One uses *Saving Private Ryan* to demonstrate the issue of actuality versus artifice in the war film and then maps this onto the history of the cinema's representation of war from the first combat documentaries, such as *The Battle of the Somme*, to the emergence of 'virtual war' in the media coverage of the Gulf War, Bosnia and Kosovo. The chapter reveals a tension between the desire to capture 'real' or 'authentic' images of war and the tendency to aestheticize war through aspects of film form and style. It maps different trajectories within the war film from the semi-documentary films of the Second World War to the spectacular international epics of the 1960s and '70s. And it also examines different national schools: the austere style of British war films of the 1940s and '50s, for example, contrasts with the 'poetic' visual stylization of Polish and Russian films of the period. I have also made reference to some films that would fall outside a narrow definition of the war film: the formal principles of structuring a battlefield evident in historical propaganda epics such as *Alexander Nevsky* and *Henry V* seem to me to have influenced the special effects-enhanced fantasy of *The Lord of the Rings*.

Chapter Two examines the representation of war as tragedy, taking as its starting point the Russian film *Come and See*, which documents in stark, uncompromising detail the horrors and atrocities of the Second World War in Belorussia. The title of the film raises once again the idea of war as spectacle, demonstrating a tension between exposing the unpleasant reality of war whilst inviting us to watch it. The chapter then maps out a history of the anti-war film, arguing that its conventions and iconography were determined by the Western Front during the First World War. It draws upon the idea of 'popular memory' or 'cultural memory' to demonstrate the extent to which war narratives are determined by national contexts. Here it is significant that whereas a memory of the First World War is shared across different societies, suggesting that the historical experience of the war is to some extent international, films of the Second World War tend to be nationally specific. Whereas the dominant Anglo-American view of the war against Nazi Germany characterizes it as the 'good war', German and Polish films, for example, offer a much more complex and ambiguous response, determined largely by specific national political and cultural circumstances. For American cinema, however, the 'bad war' is Vietnam: films examining the moral chaos of the Vietnam War reveal the extent to which the conventions of the combat film can be used for different ideological ends.

Such is the visual and emotional power of the historical lineage of anti-war cinema – *All Quiet on the Western Front*, *La Grande Illusion*, *The Red Badge of Courage*, *Kanal*, *Paths of Glory*, *Apocalypse Now* – that it has tended to obscure the existence of an alternative tradition that represents war as an adventure. Films such as *The Guns of Navarone*, *The Great Escape* and *Where Eagles Dare* may not win many accolades but they have nevertheless proved successful with cinema-goers and have endured in the popular memory of the war film.[8] Chapter Three therefore explores films belonging to what has been called 'the pleasure culture of war': the representation of war as an adventure narrative and a site of heroic actions. From the propaganda films of the two World Wars to the daredevil heroics of *Top Gun*, popular cinema has been responsible for projecting positive images of the military for public consumption. The war-as-adventure film finds its enduring form in the 'men on a mission' narrative that emerged during the Second World War and still persists in the shape of films such as *Three Kings* and the SAS biopics *Bravo Two Zero* and *The One That Got Away*. My case study here is *Rambo*, which I argue, perhaps controversially, is far from being the ideologically irredeemable exploitation cinema of popular reputation, but can be seen as a classical action film whose popularity owed less to its hawkish politics than it did to the traditional pleasures associated with the genre. And, again, I have included films from other genres: space operas such as *Star Wars* and *Starship Troopers*, for example, adopt many of the narrative and visual conventions of the combat film.

To some extent, of course, all categorization is arbitrary. It would have been as easy to write about, say, *The Great Escape* as an example of war-as-spectacle as it was to include it in the chapter on war-as-adventure, or to place *Apocalypse Now* within the context of 'men on a mission', rather than using it as an example of the moral confusion of war. The downbeat narrative and tragic conclusion of *The Victors* clearly mark it as an anti-war film, though it is included here in the context of the adventure film since it also seems a companion piece to Carl Foreman's previous film, *The Guns of Navarone*. This again underlines the extent to which my categories are fluid and flexible rather than rigid and exclusive. Inevitably, many films have been omitted: in particular documentary films from Frank Capra's *Why We Fight* series to Michael Moore's *Fahrenheit 9/11*, which do not fit easily into any particularly category. This is regrettable but necessary, however, in a book that attempts to impose some coherence onto a wide field rather than simply becoming a list or catalogue.

This book is different from others I have written in so far as it is less a work of film history than an attempt to provide a conceptual framework for approaching the subject. I have not provided fully documented production and reception histories of all the films discussed and have not included contextual information about film-makers or studios except where I felt it was absolutely necessary. Partly this is due to the confines of length and partly it is a conscious decision to focus on the issue of representation in the films. I have focused for the most part on American, British and European films that readers will be most likely to have seen or will be able to see: regrettably, and again for reasons of space, I have not included films from Asia or the Middle East. I should add, finally, that what concerns me here is to map the contours of the three lineages that I have identified: I am not making any assumption about the aesthetic or cultural value of the films themselves. In this context it seems entirely appropriate to pay equal attention to films such as the much-despised *Rambo* as to accepted classics such as *All Quiet on the Western Front*. For my own part I would gladly contend that, for example, *Where Eagles Dare* is a better film than *Apocalypse Now* or that the now largely forgotten *Nine Men* is as good a combat film as the celebrated *Saving Private Ryan*. That, however, is not the aim of this book. Instead, I have attempted to chart, as objectively as possible, the different ways in which war has been represented in popular cinema. What emerges is a picture of an enduring fascination with the subject of war and a wide and diverse range of images and narratives through which war has been served up for the edification and entertainment of the public.

1 war as spectacle

d-day redux

It is the *Citizen Kane* of war movies. Janet Maslin of the *New York Times* was speaking for many of her fellow critics when she acclaimed *Saving Private Ryan* (1998) as 'the finest war movie of our time'.[1] The film won a clutch of international critics' awards and the director, Steven Spielberg, was presented with his second Academy Award, though, like *Citizen Kane*, the film itself lost out in the Best Picture category.[2] Unlike *Citizen Kane*, however, it was a massive popular success, with a worldwide box-office gross of $480 million.[3] There are two factors that elevate *Saving Private Ryan* above the genre that it has come to define: the extent of its international success (more than half its revenues came from outside North America) and the realism of its battle scenes (an aspect widely commented upon in reviews of the film). It was, significantly, praised by veterans' organizations for representing warfare in a manner far removed from the Errol Flynnery or John Waynery of so many Hollywood treatments of war – a response that must have pleased Spielberg, who had declared his aim 'to resensitize audiences to how bad it was for the men who survived, as well as for those who perished'.[4]

Critical commentary on *Saving Private Ryan* has invariably focused on one sequence: the reconstruction of the US landings

Saving Private Ryan (Steven Spielberg, 1998).

on Omaha Beach (Dog Green Sector) on the morning of 6 June 1944. From the fade-in of waves breaking against anti-tank obstacles to the closing overhead shot of the beach strewn with the bodies of dead soldiers, this sequence comprises just over 23

minutes of a film whose total running time is 163 minutes. Its impact, however, is so vivid, and the experience of seeing it so intense, that it remains most viewers' abiding memory of the film. In these 23 minutes of screen time Spielberg created a moment

Saving Private Ryan

of film history that deserves its place alongside Eisenstein's Odessa steps, Ford's stagecoach chase and Kurosawa's rain-swept samurai battle in the pantheon of great movie action sequences. It is difficult to describe in words the sheer visual and visceral power of the sequence as flesh is ripped by machine-gun bullets, bodies are hurled into the air by explosions, limbs torn apart, brains and intestines spill onto the sand. One dazed soldier, having lost an arm, bends down to pick it up. As the men caught in this carnage fight their way ashore confusion reigns as more of them are cut down by enemy fire. Yet slowly, inexorably, they inch their way forward; an officer and his sergeant rally their men and take control; the enemy defences are breached with bangalore torpedoes and the attacking troops swarm through the gap; the enemy positions are overrun and those trapped inside killed by grenades and flame-throwers; several German soldiers are shot

whilst holding their hands in the air in the recognized position of surrender. The officer whom we have followed through the maelstrom sits down and unscrews the top of his water canteen; his hand is trembling. A long shot of the beach shows it strewn with the bodies of the dead, and the breaking waves are red with blood.

Saving Private Ryan was immediately claimed 'as Hollywood's most grimly realistic and historically accurate depiction of a World War II battlefield'.[5] This was a view widely shared amongst critics, cinema-goers, veterans and historians. Roger Ebert in the *Chicago Sun-Times* thought it 'as graphic as any war footage I've ever seen'.[6] Geoff Brown in *The Times* wrote that it displayed 'a degree of hard detail unprecedented in fictional cinema'.[7] Alexander Walker in the *Evening Standard* felt that it showed 'war as one has never seen it before on screen and hopes never to see it again'.[8] A cautionary note was sounded by *Sight and Sound* reviewer John Wrathall: 'It's meaningless for critics to write of "realism" in war movies, as most of us have no idea of what war really looks like.' Nevertheless, he found the battle sequences 'utterly believable, horrifyingly graphic in their depiction of death and injury, but somehow matter of fact, so that the worst atrocities are glimpsed out of the corner of one's eye and the choreography never shows'.[9] One of the most revealing responses to the film came from a veteran of the US Marine Corps who had experienced beach landings in the Pacific during the Second World War: 'I have never seen combat portrayed so realistically in any other war film I have seen during 60+ years of moviegoing.'[10] The US Veteran Affairs Department in Washington, DC, reported that it had received calls from D-Day veterans affected by 'powerful memories being reawakened' after seeing the film.[11] Leading military historians in Britain and America

Saving Private Ryan.

also praised the film's representation of combat. John Keegan, author of *Six Armies in Normandy* (1982), felt that it exhibited 'historical truth' in depicting the emotions of fighting – 'not only fear, which is paramount and pervasive, but also the exultation of combat and the terrible rage that can grip men suddenly released from terror in the face of an enemy who lays down his arms too late'.[12] And Stephen E. Ambrose, author of *D-Day, 6 June, 1944* (1994) and military adviser to the film, testified to the effect that *Saving Private Ryan* 'catches what happened exactly. It is, without question, the most accurate and realistic depiction of war on screen that I have ever seen.'[13]

Publicity material around the film, and Spielberg himself in promotional interviews, asserted the lengths to which the film-makers had gone to achieve this degree of realism.[14] The principal actors spent ten days in boot camp undergoing basic military training, while the extras comprised present or former servicemen who were equipped to choreograph the action sequences. With a rather ghoulish adherence to authenticity, Spielberg insisted upon using real-life amputees for the men who lost limbs in the battle. While the use of military advisers and real servicemen in war films is not in itself unusual, *Saving Private Ryan* differentiated itself from other war films through its unusual attention to both aural and visual authenticity. Thus, for example, in order to simulate the aural effect of bullets ripping into bodies, the sound editor recorded the noise of rounds being fired into meat carcasses wrapped in cloth – using the same calibre of ammunition as in 1944. The *mise-en-scène*, furthermore, replicates the 'look' of actuality combat footage from the Second World War: desaturated colours, jerky camera movements, shots out of focus, water and blood splashing the lens. Spielberg's model here was the colour combat footage in wartime US combat documentaries such as *With the Marines at Tarawa* (1944) and *The Battle of San Pietro* (1945).[15] In order to achieve this effect, Spielberg and his cameraman Janusz Kaminski used desaturated colours to replicate the appearance of combat film, removed the protective coatings from the camera lens and abandoned the usual Steadicam in favour of an image shaker that caused the camera to vibrate when explosions went off. The use of these techniques, Kaminski averred, 'created a definite sense of reality and urgency'.[16]

The effect on the spectator of these techniques is overwhelming. It is not unknown for viewers to feel physically unwell from the disorienting camerawork and the gory scenes of blood and intestines. One contributor to the American Popular Culture

Discussion List hosted by H-NET, for example, spoke of the 'nausea' induced by watching the film, testifying that 'the editing of the battle scenes had a bizarre effect on me. By the end of the Omaha Beach scene, I was feeling distinctly unwell.'[17] Another recurring feature of the response to *Saving Private Ryan* is the sense of 'being there' in the midst of the battle. 'What I like about the movie,' added one historian to the discussion, 'is that hundreds of thousands of people will for 25 minutes feel what it was like to be fighting in a war.'[18] A reviewer on the Internet Movie Database wrote that 'you will have the opportunity to participate in the D-Day operation and experience the horror of it'.[19] And even Jeanine Basinger, author of *The World War II Combat Movie* (1986), felt that the effect of the film was 'to place each and every member of the audience directly into the combat experience'.[20]

At this point we would do well to pause and remember Samuel Fuller's dictum that the only way for cinema audiences to experience what it was like to be involved in combat would be to fire live ammunition at people sitting in the movie theatre. Some film theorists, partly reacting against the extravagant claims made on behalf of *Saving Private Ryan*, argued that far from being an authentic representation of the experience of battle, it was entirely constructed, and therefore inauthentic. Spielberg's use of special-effects technology features prominently in this critique. Robert Kolker, for example, asserts that 'through the creation of animated digital bullets, flying into the screen space, towards the soldiers from an unseen enemy, the viewer is given the opportunity to share the anxiety (if not the danger) of battle'. The effect

The Army Film and Photographic Unit.

of this 'theme-park style' ride, Kolker suggests, is ultimately 'not so different from *Jurassic Park*'.[21] In this interpretation the emphasis is not on realism but on spectacle: what the film offers is not the reality of war but a sensory simulation of it. In this way the spectator is allowed to experience the thrill (or nausea) of battle but without the inconvenience of actually being shot or blown to pieces. In this sense, so the argument goes, *Saving Private Ryan* is no more realistic than a video or computer game.

Whether or not one accepts this argument – and my opinion is that to compare *Saving Private Ryan* to a video game is to trivialize its content by focusing solely on its technique – there is, nevertheless, an irony in the fact that the perceived realism of the film is achieved largely through artifice. *Saving Private Ryan* is the creation of a master film-maker with all the technical expertise and resources of a major Hollywood studio at his disposal. There is a sense in which its close-up scenes of carnage on the beaches are 'more real' than could ever have been captured by a

cameraman at the time. A comparison of the Omaha Beach sequence of *Saving Private Ryan* and actuality film taken by Allied service cameramen is instructive in this regard. Toby Haggith of the Imperial War Museum's Film Archive has demonstrated that Spielberg's pastiche of the style of combat footage was based on films of the Pacific theatre rather than

Normandy (there is no colour film of the beach landings, for example) and that he includes shots that would have been obviously impossible for service cameramen to achieve (such as the image of the first casualties, machine-gunned immediately after the ramp of their landing craft is lowered, but taken from outside the landing craft looking back towards it). In fact, the conditions experienced by the army cameramen on D-Day militated against capturing anything like the dramatic imagery that Spielberg was able to create 53 years later. Haggith concedes that 'the Spielberg version of D-Day is a more impressive account of the event', but concludes that the differences between *Saving Private Ryan* and actuality footage highlights 'the artificial and manipulative technique with which the battle has been recreated'.[22]

To recognize Spielberg's 'artificial and manipulative technique' is to locate *Saving Private Ryan* within debates in film studies between realist and formative approaches to the medium. The realist approach, whose most influential proponent was the French critic André Bazin, is posited on the assumption that film is at its most realistic when it resembles closely external physical reality. In his essay 'The Myth of Total Cinema', for example, Bazin argued that the film medium was characterized by 'an integral realism, a recreation of the world in its own image, an image unburdened by the freedom of the artist or the irreversibility of time'.[23] He admired the Italian Neo-realist cinema of the late 1940s, which he considered artistically superior to previous film styles on account of its aesthetic realism and emotional truth. The formative approach, in contrast, contends that the true artistry of the film medium lies in its ability to manipulate the image for aesthetic effect. Rudolf Arnheim, for instance, argued that the formal components of a film 'show themselves able to do more than simply reproduce the required object; they sharpen it, impose a style upon it, point out special features, make it vivid and decorative'. 'Art begins where mechanical reproduction leaves off,' Arnheim asserted, 'where conditions of representation serve in some way to mould the object.'[24] To this end formative theorists champion the montage school of Soviet cinema in the 1920s, which applied scientific principles to the technique of editing and privileged the formal systems of film over and above the unmediated image.

With its use of montage editing and its fragmented *mise-en-scène*, the Omaha Beach sequence of *Saving Private Ryan* clearly belongs in the formative tradition. This is not to say that those commentators who acclaimed it for its realism are wrong – far from it – but rather that the sort of realism it represents is not of the Bazinian variety. Clearly, it does not conform to Bazin's ideal model of long takes and depth of field: the editing is rapid and the image is often out of focus. In fact, Spielberg employs non-realistic devices, including slow-motion and unsynchronous sound effects (to represent Captain Miller's temporary disorientation), which are the antithesis of Bazin's notion of realism. It is perhaps more useful to see *Saving Private Ryan* as part of a trend, along with other special effects-enhanced blockbusters of the 1990s, including *Jurassic Park* and *Titanic*, towards what has been termed 'hyper-realism'. More usually associated with fantasy and science fiction, hyper-realism refers to an emphasis on realistic detail achieved through special effects. In *Saving Private Ryan* special-effects technology is used to create otherwise impossible images of the impact of bullets and bombs on men's bodies. In this regard *Saving Private Ryan* 'undeniably marks an epistemological break in the mimesis of violence, a process central to modern Western culture'.[25]

It would probably be more accurate to describe the realism of *Saving Private Ryan* as mimetic rather than aesthetic in that its fictional characters act and behave in a way that we find plausible. To this extent the film exhibits realist characteristics as defined by John Ellis: that a film or television narrative 'should have a surface accuracy; it should conform to notions of what we expect to happen; it should explain itself adequately to us as audience; it should conform to particular notions of psychology and character motivation'.[26] In this sense realism is a set of representational conventions that conform to our expectations of what an event should be like. The irony here is that our perceptions of what D-Day was like have been shaped largely by other films. It is always likely, of course, that some cinema-goers may have read histories of D-Day by writers such as Stephen Ambrose (*D-Day, 6 June, 1944*) and Cornelius Ryan (*The Longest Day*), but it is equally likely that many more will have seen Darryl F. Zanuck's film of *The Longest Day* (1962) than will have read the book on which it was based. Realism, to quote Ellis again, 'represents the spectator's desire that a representation should conform to common sense and taken-for-granted notions of events . . . it demands that the Second World War is shown as a conflict with the virtuous Allies pitted against satanic Germans and sub-human Japanese'.[27] This is the familiar narrative of the Second

Saving Private Ryan.

World War presented by most Hollywood treatments of the subject. In this regard it could be argued that *Saving Private Ryan* is realistic not so much because it represents what the Second World War was like but rather because it conforms to our expectations of what a Second World War combat movie should be. Or, as one commentator puts it, 'the history of the war film might prove a better context for understanding *Saving Private Ryan*'s achievement than the history of the War itself'.[28]

Perhaps one of the factors that explain the elevated status of *Saving Private Ryan* in the history of combat films is that it represents almost a compendium of the genre. It is 'filled with appropriations from and allusions to a genre it both emulates and calls into question'.[29] Those allusions are too many to list in detail here; a few examples will suffice to demonstrate the visual and narrative references that *Saving Private Ryan* makes to other genre films. Thus the screen-filling image of the Stars and Stripes that opens and closes the film immediately brings to mind *Patton* (1970). (Some critics have suggested that the patriotic imagery of *Saving Private Ryan* compromises its status as an anti-war film. My own assessment is that the film is not, nor was it intended to be, an anti-war film.) The beach assault and the burning of enemy pill boxes with flame-throwers recalls similar scenes in *Sands of Iwo Jima* (1949), while the slow-motion deaths would seem to have been a conscious visual allusion to *Cross of Iron* (1977). The soldier who loses his rifle on the beach and the breaching of the German defences with bangalore torpedoes (long tubes packed with explosives) are both incidents borrowed directly from *The Longest Day*. The main narrative of *Saving Private Ryan* – Captain Miller leads a squad into Normandy to find and extract a paratrooper whose brothers have all been killed in action – adheres to the conventions of the patrol movie established by films such as *A Walk in the Sun* (1945). The characterization of Captain Miller (Tom Hanks) is partly modelled on Captain Wilson (Robert Mitchum) in *The Story of GI Joe* (1945), while Southern sharpshooter Private Jackson bears affinities with Gary Cooper's Alvin York in *Sergeant York* (1941). In common with both *The Story of GI Joe* and *Sands of Iwo Jima*, the central protagonist of *Saving Private Ryan* dies at the film's climax. While the story itself is fictional, there were several instances during the Second World War of brothers killed in action: the most tragic example were the Sullivan brothers who all perished when the USS *Juneau* was sunk in the Pacific. Their story was dramatized in *The Sullivans* (1944), from which *Saving Private Ryan* borrows a scene of the men's mother receiving the telegram informing her of their deaths. Finally, the second major battle sequence at the end of the film – the defence of a strategically important bridge against a German counter-attack – makes conscious reference to the popular narrative of American history when Miller refers to their last bastion as 'The Alamo'.

There are many other aspects of *Saving Private Ryan* worthy of comment, including, but not limited to, its representation of masculinity and comradeship, its relationship to the culture of commemoration and remembrance, and its promotion of the Second World War as 'the good war' in response to the cycle of Vietnam films that adopted a more or less anti-war ideological position.[30] Nor should it be assumed that its popular reputation as 'the greatest war movie' is uncontested. Derek Malcolm, for one, felt that 'to suggest that it may be the best war film of all time, as someone already has, is either hyperbole or plain ignorance. What about Lewis Milestone's *All Quiet on the Western Front*, Stanley Kubrick's *Paths of Glory*, Gillo Pontecorvo's *The Battle of Algiers* or Jean Renoir's *La Grande Illusion*?'[31] Yet just as *Citizen Kane* (1941) provides a textbook example of the application of realist and formative film theories – long takes and deep-focus cinematography on the one hand, expressionist lighting and montage sequences on the other – so *Saving Private Ryan* offers us an entry into many of the issues that have informed the representation of war in film. The critical and popular response to the film demonstrates a tension between realism and spectacle that has been a consistent feature of responses to war and film since the early history of the medium.

the cinematograph goes to war

One of the H-NET discussants on *Saving Private Ryan*, a Vietnam War veteran with combat experience, revealed that the film's sound effects 'forced me to duck a little as I perceived bullets whizzing past my head'.[32] Ninety years earlier, in 1898, a travelling film showman averred that when he showed a topical news film of the Spanish–American War, 'the pictures of battleships in action were so real that every time a shot was fired the women would duck their heads to let the thirteen-inch shells pass over'.[33] Both these anecdotes are illuminating for what they reveal about the nature of spectatorship and the illusion of reality created by film. At the end of the nineteenth century this response could be explained by the novelty and unfamiliarity of seeing moving pictures – just as Parisian audiences are reported to have leapt from their seats when confronted with the Lumières' *L'arrivé d'un train en garet*. At the end of the twentieth century, when cinema audiences had become more sophisticated in their reading and decoding of images, this reaction is more surprising, but the effect on the spectator is much the same even if the technology that achieves it has changed.

Until the advent of photography no one who had not experienced war at first hand could possibly know what it was really like. Before the mid-nineteenth century, impressions of war came from returning soldiers, from dispatches in newspapers and from drawings and paintings that more than likely adopted a highly stylized, romanticized image of warfare. The Crimean War (1854–6) is the first for which photographic evidence is available, though even so it was the dispatches of William Howard Russell, the first war correspondent as we understand the term today, that did more to reveal the inefficient conduct of the war to the British public than the efforts of the royal photographer Roger Fenton, who was sent to the Crimea in a bid to provide counter-propaganda against the highly critical reports in the press. There is a substantial photographic record of the American Civil War (1861–5), where the Union hired Alexander Gardner as the official photographer for the 'Army of the Potomac'. Advertisements for exhibitions of Gardner's photographs declared that they 'bring the battle fields, their incidents and localities, before us in the most faithful and vivid manner'.[34] It was only towards the turn of the century, however, that visual records of war received widespread dissemination through the invention of cinematography. The cinematograph was, as Pierre Sorlin puts it, 'a younger sibling of photography'.[35] The Spanish–American War (1898) and the Anglo–Boer War (1899–1902) were the first to be covered by cinematographers and short 'actualities' of war scenes were one of the first types of genre film.

Much of the initial appeal of moving pictures was that they offered, or at least seemed to offer, images of the real world. Film was heralded as a medium of pictorial reproduction that was synonymous with the events it demonstrated. In 1898, for example, the Polish pioneer film-maker Boleslaw Matuszewski anticipated Bazin's critical writings by half a century when he remarked: 'The cinematograph may not give a complete history, but what it gives is incontestably and absolutely true.'[36] It is perhaps only to be expected that early film-makers would make such claims for their own work: they were businessmen first and artists second. The 'actuality' was the dominant genre of early film production. As well as filming scenes of everyday life, the pioneer cinematographers soon turned their cameras on historical events: early examples of such 'topicals' include the coronation of Tsar Nicholas II (1896) and the funeral procession of Queen Victoria (1901). Yet it is now apparent that many early topicals purporting to show historical events were in fact dramatic reconstructions. As well as famous 'trick' films such as *Le voyage dans la lune*, for example, the French pioneer Georges Méliès also specialized in reconstructions of newsworthy events such as the sinking of the battleship USS *Maine* (1898) and the assassination of US President William McKinley (1901). The first example of a battlefield reconstruction passed off as the real thing is probably the Vitagraph Company's *The Battle of Santiago Bay* (1898). The cinematographer, Albert E. Smith, travelled to Cuba and shot some actuality footage, but when it was considered not to be dramatic enough Smith and his partner, J. Stuart Blackton, faked the battle using a water tank, cardboard ships and smoke from their cigars. When this was mixed with authentic actuality material, it seems that audiences did not detect the fake.[37] To be fair to early film-makers, their intention was not necessarily to deceive and the fact that their films were reconstructed was sometimes acknowledged. The British pioneer R. W. Paul, for example, produced a series of topicals entitled *Reproductions of Incidents of the Boer War* and claimed that they had been 'arranged under the supervision of an experienced military officer from the front'.[38]

The advent of cinematography in the 1890s was part of a communications revolution that also saw the emergence of the mass-circulation popular press (exemplified in Britain by Lord Northcliffe's *Daily Mail* and in America by William Randolph Hearst's 'yellow press') and the invention of wireless telegraphy. The convergence of these media made it possible to report news events quickly and to disseminate images to a wide section of the general public. It was during the Anglo-Boer War that the potential of the mass media for propaganda and counter-propaganda was first recognized. The popular press became increasingly jingoistic in reporting events in South Africa, and celebrity authors such as Winston Churchill and Arthur Conan Doyle published eyewitness accounts of the war as counter-propaganda against the negative reports appearing overseas, especially in Germany. Cinematographers also travelled to South Africa, notably William Dickson of the British Mutoscope and Biograph Company, who published a memoir of his experiences as *The Biograph in Battle*.[39] Much of the footage that Dickson shot can legitimately be described as actuality – scenes of troops in camp and on the move – though even so many shots were evidently staged for the camera. British soldiers were dressed in Boer uniforms to reconstruct skirmishes, and it was reported that the British commander-in-chief, Lord Roberts, 'consented to be biographed with all his Staff, actually having his table taken out into the sun for the convenience of Mr Dickson'.[40]

The cinematograph was at the heart of what Simon Popple, historian of early popular visual culture, has described as a 'representational nexus' that provided 'a new technological iconography of the war, a new form of evidence considered far more legitimate than that of the war correspondent or the special artist'.[41] Hereafter the demand for visual representations of war would exceed that for the more traditional written dispatches. To this extent the Boer War may be said to represent the start of a process through which images from the front have been disseminated to the public. The television coverage of the Vietnam and Gulf wars can be seen in a direct line of descent from the films shot by Dickson and others in South Africa. The technology has changed, but the cameraman 'at the front' remains the principal means of reporting war for the news media.

It was during the First World War that the cinematograph came of age as a medium of war reporting. The necessity, during total war, of each side projecting its war effort to publics both at home and abroad in order to maintain morale and influence opinion brought about the organization of official propaganda agencies to facilitate this. Most of the belligerent nations allowed cinematographers access to the front, though, initially at least, they were not always welcomed by the military authorities. There are uncanny similarities between the British and German experiences, where the history was one of initial scepticism at the beginning of the war to grudging acceptance by around 1916, followed by a belated recognition of the value of the cinematograph by the war's end. The antipathy of the War Office towards the film industry meant that there was no official film of the British army during the first eighteen months of the war. It was not until late in 1915 that the Topical Committee for War Films was established, following much lobbying by the trade, which was desperate to secure actuality film from the front to meet public demand. An official newsreel, the *War Office Topical Budget*, was set up in 1917 by Lord Beaverbrook, the press baron brought into the government by Lloyd George. In 1918 the appointments of Beaverbrook as Minister of Information and of Sir William Jury, a leading distributor-exhibitor, as Director of the Cinematograph Propaganda Department effectively put the trade in charge of film propaganda. In Germany, too, military authorities were hostile towards film-makers and early efforts were hampered by restricted access to the front. In 1916 a film and photography unit was appended to the army's liaison office. In 1917 this unit was reconstituted as BUFA (Bild- und Filmamt) and was responsible to the General Staff. BUFA established several military (rather than civilian) film units to take actuality film at the front. By this time no less a figure than General Erich Ludendorff had been converted to the view that 'the war has demonstrated the paramount power of images and of film as means of enlightenment and influence'.[42] Ludendorff supported the establishment of the giant consortium UFA (Universum Film Aktiengesellschaft) at the end of 1917, though it had little opportunity to make any significant impact before the collapse of the Western Front in the summer of 1918. When the United States entered the war in 1917, it immediately set up a Committee on Public Information, while the US Army Signal Corps was designated as its official film unit. The Americans were quicker to recognize the value of cinematography, though they had less opportunity to put it into practice than the European powers.

While there is a quite extensive film record of the war, however, its quality is patchy. Sorlin contends that much of the actuality footage of the war 'is tediously repetitive, mostly parades, long lines of prisoners, or tracking-shots of the seemingly inexhaustible build-up of supplies accumulated before offensives'.[43] This also seems to have been the response of those who saw the films. British audiences were disappointed by early films of the Western Front because they did not contain any close, dramatic footage of the fighting.[44] The German trade paper *Der Kinematograph* complained that 'hardly anything can be recognized clearly. The distances are immense, the sharpshooters in the trenches are hard to discern, and the whole field of battle gives the impression of a landscape that is almost completely dead.'[45] During the first two years of the war, especially, films gave little impression of the reality of war and tended to consist of scenes behind the lines or shots of the aftermath of battle. The dramatization of acts of brutality by the enemy was a regular feature of films on both sides – a form of atrocity propaganda that seems to have been successful in arousing hatred.

All this changed in 1916 with the release of *The Battle of the Somme*. As it happened, the first major British official film of the war came about unintentionally. In June 1916 two cameramen, Geoffrey Malins and J. B. McDowell, were sent to film the British Fourth Army launching its offensive along the River Somme. They filmed the artillery bombardment and troops marching through villages behind the lines. On the morning of 1 July Malins filmed the explosion of a giant mine under the German redoubt at Hawthorn Ridge, before following men of the 1st Lancashire Fusiliers moving up through the approach trenches. He was unable to film the actual assault, in which the

The Battle of the Somme (Geoffrey Malins and J. B. McDowell, 1916).

Fusiliers sustained heavy casualties in the face of the German machine-gunners, so instead he joined his colleague McDowell at a first-aid station, where they filmed the wounded of both sides being treated. They also shot film of captured German trenches and, finally, the survivors of the first wave assault coming out of the line to rest. The first rushes of the material shot by Malins and McDowell were shown to members of the Topical Committee in London a week and a half later, whereupon it was decided that the footage should be edited into a full-length film. *The Battle of the Somme* was released in London on 21 August and followed in other major cities a week later.[46]

The contemporary response to *The Battle of the Somme* has been well documented. It evidently made an enormous impact on the British public: there were reports of hundreds of thousands of people flocking to see it, and it received what effectively amounted to an official endorsement when George V saw it at Windsor. Reviews of the film were enthusiastic, commenting on its vivid and realistic images of the front. The trade journal *Bioscope*, for example, declared that

> no written description by an eyewitness, however graphic his pen; no illustration by any artist, no matter how facile his pencil; no verbal description by the most interested participator in the event, could hope to convey to the man at home the reality of modern warfare with the force and conviction shown in this marvellous series of pictures.[47]

There were some, however, who found the spectacle of war distressing, feeling that shots of dead Tommies were inappropriate and distasteful. The Dean of Durham wrote to *The Times* to protest that

> crowds of Londoners feel no scruple at feasting their eyes on pictures which present the passion and death of British

soldiers in *Battle of the Somme* . . . I beg leave respectfully to enter a protest against an entertainment which wounds the hearts and violates the very sanctities of bereavement.[48]

A more balanced response came from the author Sir Henry Rider Haggard, who wrote in his diary that the film

> does give a wonderful idea of the fighting . . . The most impressive [shot] to my mind is that of a regiment scrambling out of a trench to charge and of the one man who slides back shot dead. There is something appalling about the instantaneous change from fierce activity to supine death.[49]

The irony here is that the sequence in *The Battle of the Somme* that provoked these reactions – as Roger Smither has conclusively demonstrated – is not authentic.[50] An inter-title declares: 'The attack. At a signal, along the entire 16 mile front, the British troops leaped over the trench parapets and advanced towards the German trenches, under heavy fire of the enemy.' The film shows a dozen men leaving their trench and going 'over the top'; two fall back and lie face-down on the slope of the trench. A low-angle shot from a different position then shows troops advancing through barbed wire; again two of them fall. A close scrutiny of the sequence, however, reveals that these scenes were staged for the camera at some distance from the front line. The trench is shallow and there is no barbed wire to protect it; the troops are not wearing backpacks or carrying any equipment

The Battle of the Somme.

other than their rifles; and the position of the camera is dangerously exposed, especially in the shot of the men advancing into
what is supposed to be No Man's Land. The clinching detail is
that one of the soldiers who is shot, apparently dead, and falls
onto the barbed wire can be seen afterwards crossing his legs in
order to make himself more comfortable. There are other incon-
sistencies in *The Battle of the Somme*, including the uniforms
worn by the troops and details such as protective covers over the
weapons of men about to go into battle, that suggest scenes were
staged specifically for the camera. The evidence of staged scenes
notwithstanding, however, Smither argues that *The Battle of the
Somme* should still be regarded as an authentic document of war
on the grounds that 'the proportion of such film to the whole
work is actually quite small'.[51]

   While the two films are very different in form and style,
there are, nevertheless, some useful points of comparison
between *The Battle of the Somme* and *Saving Private Ryan*. Both
films purport to show the reality of war; both resort to trickery to
do so. In *The Battle of the Somme* the 'fake' sequences are quite
unsophisticated, certainly in comparison to Spielberg's elabo-
rately staged pyrotechnics, but the principle behind them is much
the same: to make the audience feel they have seen war, even experienced it, at close quarters. The contemporary response to both
films, furthermore, is remarkably similar: viewers were impressed
(in some cases shocked) by their graphic and apparently realistic
images of the battlefield. Nicholas Reeves, in his study of the
reception of *The Battle of the Somme*, concluded that

millions of men, women and children who made up the domestic cinema audience in the summer of 1916 believed that in viewing *Battle of the Somme* they had seen the face of modern war for the very first time. We concentrate on the extent of faking in the film; contemporaries were struck by its honesty, by its realism, by its truthfulness.[52]

Similarly, as we have seen, while some commentators have suggested that the techniques used to recreate the combat scenes in *Saving Private Ryan* render them artificial, audiences and critics perceived them to be real.

Which of the films, however, is the more authentic? In so far as *The Battle of the Somme* is compiled from actuality footage shot at the front – even the 'fakes' are closer to the real thing than Spielberg's mocked-up combat film – then it should probably be regarded as more authentic than *Saving Private Ryan*. That said, however, *The Battle of the Somme* gives no indication of the extent of casualties suffered by the British on the first day of the Somme (some 20,000 dead and nearly twice that number wounded), whereas *Saving Private Ryan* virtually wallows in the carnage of Omaha Beach (where some 3,000 Americans lost their lives and half as many again were wounded). This, of course, is due to the different historical contexts of the films: the former a propaganda film intended to persuade the British public that the war on the Western Front was going well, the latter a commemoration of the sacrifice made by a generation of young Americans 'on the altar of freedom'. It is perhaps only to be expected, therefore, that *The Battle of the Somme* would omit the fact of heavy casualties, whereas in *Saving Private Ryan* the losses sustained at the beginning of the film are essential to its ideological project. These differences in intent are just as significant to the ways in which the two films picture war as are the technological differences between them.

For all its flaws, *The Battle of the Somme* 'may be acclaimed in hindsight as the first feature-length British battle documentary and thus the direct ancestor of such notable Second World War films as *Desert Victory* and *The True Glory*'.[53] While the evidence would seem to suggest that contemporary audiences did not detect the reconstructed sequences, this is not to say that *The Battle of the Somme* was necessarily disingenuous. (In contrast, Malins himself made somewhat exaggerated claims of his own heroics in his published record, *How I Filmed the War*, where his description of the 'over the top' sequence is demonstrably different from what the film actually shows.)[54] At this time the issue of authenticity that so vexes historians today would not seem to have troubled either the film-makers or their audiences. Indeed, it seems to have been accepted practice to 'improve' the filmic record by recourse to reconstruction if, for technical or practical reasons, it had been impossible to achieve the shots that the cameramen wanted. This practice would persist into the inter-war period.

Most of the official film machinery was disbanded at the end of the war, though the newsreel *Topical Budget* continued until 1931. The links forged between the cinematograph industry and the military authorities remained, however, exemplified in the cycle of battle reconstructions produced by Harry Bruce

All Quiet on the Western Front (Lewis Milestone, 1930).

Woolfe for British Instructional Films – *The Battle of Jutland* (1921), *Ypres* (1925), *Mons* (1926) and *The Battles of the Coronel and Falkland Islands* (1927) – made with the cooperation of the War Office and Admiralty. Michael Paris suggests that these films reflected an official view in so far as they 'portrayed the War as a national achievement – an adventure in which brave young Britons won immortality'.[55] And the Paramount Pictures aviation epic *Wings* (1927) – perhaps the first truly spectacular war film in terms of sheer size and scope – was produced with the full cooperation of the US War Department and can be seen, rather like *Top Gun* nearly 60 years later, in the context of an official recruitment drive following the Air Corps Act of 1926.[56]

It was during the inter-war period that the news film became institutionalized with the emergence of companies such as Movietone, Gaumont and Pathé. Rivalry between newsreel organizations was one reason for the use of reconstructed footage in their coverage of events such as the Italian invasion of Abyssinia in 1935 and the Spanish Civil War, which broke out in 1936. Anthony Aldgate has demonstrated how the newsreels 'drew upon the same visual iconography of war that had always met with great success in every realm of the film industry'.[57] Thus it is that newsreel coverage would often include obviously faked images, such as shots of troops advancing *towards* the camera and close-ups of explosions that would almost certainly have resulted in the death or serious injury of any cameraman in the proximity. It was during these years, moreover, that a tradition began that persists to this day: the practice of using extracts from feature films – particularly the impressive battle sequences from *All Quiet on the Western Front* (1930) – to represent purportedly authentic images of the Western Front during the Great War.

The emergence of a rival to the newsreels in the field of actuality and non-fiction film during the 1930s, in the form of the documentary movement, brought issues of authenticity and representation to the fore. This is not the place for a survey history of the documentary film: rival claimants for the 'father' of documentary include the American Robert Flaherty, the Scot John Grierson and even the Lumière brothers of France. The differences between the documentary movement and the news-reels have generally been categorized in terms that see the docu-mentarists as progressive (politically, socially, aesthetically) and the newsreels as conservative. This categorization – accurate enough if somewhat simplistic – can be attributed in large meas-ure to the writings of John Grierson, who, if not the father of the documentary movement, was certainly its first theorist. Grierson derided newsreels for their triviality and for their lack of serious engagement with the contemporary world: they were 'dim records . . . of only the evanescent and the essentially unreal, reflecting hardly anything worth preserving of the times they recorded'.[58] The claims of the documentary movement to repre-sent reality do not, in fact, stand up to close scrutiny. The realism of films such as Grierson's *Drifters* (1929) was as much a fabrica-tion in its own right as the faked sequences in *The Battle of the*

Somme. The British documentarists of the 1930s made use of studio reconstructions and were prone to the use of 'artistic' effects. Grierson himself spoke of 'the creative treatment of actuality' and admired Soviet montage cinema of the 1920s. In fact, the differences between the documentary movement and the commercial sector of the film industry (including feature film producers as well as the newsreels) were rather less distinct than the polemical division between the two schools in the 1930s would suggest. This is evident from the ease with which practitioners from both newsreel and documentary were assimilated into the official propaganda effort during the Second World War.

The actuality film record of the Second World War is much more complete than the First: there were many more cameramen and a much more coordinated approach to filming the war. Basil Wright later remarked that combatant governments

> needed no convincing of the importance of the film-camera as a recorder – strategic as well as historical – of combat on land, sea and in the air; though the day had not yet come when a war like that in Vietnam could be fought, atrocities and all, publicly, daily and in colour in everyone's parlour.[59]

The most systematic and organized approach to filming combat operations was in Nazi Germany: several years before the outbreak of war the Ministry of Propaganda had decided to set up PK Units (Propaganda Kompanie Einheiten) that would be attached to the services. In 1939 there were thirteen of these PK Units, each with more than a hundred men, and it was due to Goebbels's faith in these 'soldier cameramen' that the Germans had a full film record of the campaigns in Poland in 1939 and in France and the Low Countries in 1940. The footage from these early campaigns was put to most effective use in the notorious 'shock and awe' documentaries *Baptism of Fire* (*Feuertaufe*, 1940) and *Victory in the West* (*Sieg im Westen*, 1941).[60] The British perspective of the war was covered both by the newsreels and by the film units of the armed services. The Army Film Unit (which became the Army Film and Photographic Unit in 1941) grew from four cameramen at the beginning of the war to eighty by 1943, organized into four sections attached to different sectors. Its early results were disappointing – most of the footage of the Dunkirk evacuation, for example, came from newsreel rather than service cameramen – though the AFPU took a more principled stance against reconstruction than the newsreels, which during the North African campaign 'became notorious for faking many sequences of combat to make newsreel and propaganda films more exciting'.[61] The Americans, following the disappointing results of their cameramen in North Africa in 1943, entirely restructured their film organization so that by 1944 they had more than 400 cameramen in the European theatre. Not only was D-Day the greatest strategic and logistical undertaking in modern warfare, but also it was 'the most lavishly equipped and planned photographic operation in history'.[62]

Apart from its value as primary source material for future historians, there were two main uses to which this actuality film was put. The first was for intelligence and training: film assisted in such matters as gauging the accuracy and effectiveness of aerial bombing and in the development of new weapons technologies. Such films were made solely for the armed forces and were often regarded as secret: British test film of weapons systems such as the 'bouncing bomb' (a misnomer used to describe the aerial mines used against the Ruhr dams in 1943) and the 'panjandrum' (a rocket-propelled giant wheel designed to clear the beaches of mines on D-Day but never put into service) remained classified for half a century after the war. The second, and most visible, role for actuality film was in the production of special combat documentaries released after the event with the aim of informing the public about the progress of the war, though, by their nature, such films tended to depict victories rather than defeats. The British produced three 'Victory' films – *Desert Victory* (1943), *Tunisian Victory* (1944) and *Burma Victory* (1945) – compiled largely from actuality film shot at the front by the AFPU. The editing of these films was carried out by feature-film directors who had joined the AFPU, such as Roy Boulting and David Macdonald. Similarly, several leading US film-makers, including John Ford, John Huston and William Wyler, joined the US Army Signal Corps and were involved in combat photography. Films such as Ford's *The Battle of Midway* (1942) and Wyler's *The Memphis Belle* (1944), in particular, were notable for their use of colour actuality film (16-millimetre or 35-millimetre Kodachrome). The Soviet Union, not to be outdone, produced *The Defeat of the German Armies near Moscow* (1942) and *The Siege of Leningrad* (1943). The Soviet film-maker Vsevolod Pudovkin believed that the genre 'is fully international and can be fully understood anywhere. The commentator's voice may be translated into any language without disturbing the integrity of impression. The montage of visual images does not require translation.'[63] While we might not accept that a translated commentary retains the same meaning as in its original form (the ideological slant of a film can be significantly changed by a commentary), Pudovkin's point about the power of the visual image remains valid. These films were also distributed in Allied territories: the Soviet films were shown in Britain and in America (where *The Defeat of the German Armies near Moscow* was retitled *Moscow Strikes Back* and featured a commentary by Edward G. Robinson) and *Desert Victory*, significant in so far as it depicted the first major British land victory of the war, was released in the United States and the Soviet Union. Stalin saw the film and cabled somewhat mischievously to Churchill: 'The film depicts magnificently how Britain is fighting, and stigmatizes those scoundrels (there are such people also in our country) who are asserting that Britain is not fighting at all, but is merely an onlooker.'[64]

The combat documentary is a form of spectacle in that it satisfies the public's desire to see war at close quarters. The promotion and reception discourses of these films would typically emphasize their authenticity: actuality footage was seen as an attraction in its own right and as a means of differentiating the combat documentary from the fiction film. The evidence would seem to suggest that audiences accepted what they saw on screen as real. *Desert Victory*, for example, was one of the favourite films of 1943 amongst the respondents to a Mass-Observation survey in

Desert Victory (David McDonald, 1943).

Britain who described it in terms such as 'factual stuff', 'pure documentary' and 'the stark reality portrayed'.[65] It is clear, however, that the practice of reconstruction persisted. In *Desert Victory*, a sequence of sappers advancing to clear a minefield at El Alamein was shot at Pinewood Studios and cut into a montage of actuality footage of a night barrage. The differences in clarity, lighting and staging make it obvious that this was shot in a studio. (This did not prevent extracts from the sequence, including both actuality and reconstructed shots, cropping up in Twentieth Century-Fox's feature film of 1951, *The Desert Fox*. Fox had distributed *Desert Victory* in North America.) In *Tunisian Victory*, a joint Anglo-American production, the reconstructed sequences are more difficult to spot because they were shot outdoors. The American attack on Hill 609 was in fact shot in the Mojave Desert in California (where the topography resembled western Tunisia), while the British crossing of the Wadi Zig-Zaou was again staged at Pinewood.

The campaign documentaries were made primarily to explain the strategic aspects of the war to the general public and to this extent they tend to make extensive use of maps and explanatory captions. Towards the end of the war, however, official film-makers were clearly attempting to engage with the human consequences of war. John Huston's *The Battle of San Pietro* was an account of the Italian campaign that gave a convincing impression of the war from the perspective of the ordinary GI. The film ran into problems with the military authorities, who insisted that Huston had removed voice-overs from 'dead' soldiers and held up its release for nearly a year. Even in its final form, however, *The Battle of San Pietro* is 'a remarkable film. The horror of war is real – dead bodies, devastated towns, shocked civilians and war-weary soldiers.'[66] The sensitivity over showing the bodies of dead soldiers that had arisen over *The Battle of the Somme* persisted. A correspondent to *The Times* deplored

> a strong tendency on the part of news-reel editors to include in their films of battle sequences close-up 'shots' of dead and mutilated bodies of enemy soldiers . . . It is all too easy to substitute mentally the bodies of our countrymen for those of the enemy, boldly, nay vengefully, shown to an audience which almost certainly contains wives and parents whose loved ones have given, or yet may give, their lives in such grim circumstances.[67]

The most successful of the combat documentaries, at least in the view of most critics, was *The True Glory* (1945). Produced

The True Glory (Carol Reed, 1945).

on behalf of SHAEF (Supreme Headquarters Allied Expeditionary Force) and supervised by a Joint Production Committee headed by Britain's Carol Reed and America's Garson Kanin, *The True Glory* is an account of the liberation of Europe, from D-Day until the surrender of the German armies in the West.[68] Where *The True Glory* is most effective is in its juxtaposition of a triumphalist commentary (written in modern blank verse by the playwright Robert E. Sherwood) with the anecdotes of individual servicemen that are by turns matter-of-fact, humorous, tragic or poignant. Through this device the film contrasts the 'official' view of the campaign from above with an 'unofficial' view from below. *The Listener* felt that 'whereas many of the earlier war documentaries composed of actual combat scenes have somehow lacked humanity – have been full of guns and tanks and explosions – *The True Glory* is primarily about people'.[69]

The True Glory represents the culmination of the combat documentary form that had begun three decades earlier with *The*

Battle of the Somme. Later wars, such as Korea and Vietnam, did not easily lend themselves to the same treatment: they were confined to a single theatre and did not progress in such a way as to allow the sermonizing of a film like *The True Glory*. And, for all their critical reputation, feature-length combat documentaries were not attractive to distributors: they were handled as part of the trade's patriotic duty but with little faith in their commercial value. Thus it was that the genre did not outlast the Second World War. And the millions of feet of actuality film of the war languished in the archives for a generation. It had been suggested, as early as 1941, that the AFPU's material should be used 'for the compilation of an exhaustive history of the war on film'.[70] It was not until a quarter of a century later, however, that this finally appeared in the form of Thames Television's 26-part documentary series *The World at War*. *The World at War* differed from previous television documentaries, such as the American-produced *Victory at Sea* and *Crusade in Europe*, in that it was compiled from unedited actuality film held by the archives rather than using only the commercial newsreel libraries. The production team embarked upon what, at the time, was the most extensive research in the film archives (though they were denied access to Soviet and East German sources) and, led by the producer, Jeremy Isaacs, were at pains to ensure that they used only actuality film and not reconstruction. Isaacs impressed upon the production team that 'we are not making "poetic" films with licence to use footage where we please. We are making an historic series and should not knowingly use pictures purporting to be what they are not.'[71] *The World at War* was broadcast to great acclaim in 1973–4 and set new standards for television documentary production based on archival materials.

The professional discourse of programmes such as *The World at War* posits a clear distinction between actuality and reconstruction. Yet, by the 1960s and '70s this distinction was again becoming blurred. This was a consequence, in part, of intellectual developments in the academy: the radicalization of French film culture following the upheavals of 1968 and the ascendancy of high theory in journals such as *Screen* after *circa* 1970 signalled a rejection of the Bazinian orthodoxy in favour of the idea that all film was merely a 'representation' or 'construction' and had no claim to objective reality. (To be fair to Bazin, he had recognized this himself in his observation that 'realism in art can only be achieved in one way – through artifice'. This was a point his critics tend to overlook.) In the realms of practice, meanwhile, films such as Kevin Brownlow's and Andrew Mollo's *It Happened Here* (1963) and Gillo Pontecorvo's *The Battle of Algiers* (*La battaglia di Algeri*, 1965) had complicated the notions of actuality and authenticity in new ways. *It Happened Here* was a documentary-style account of an event that never happened: an 'alternate history' of what might have happened if Britain had been invaded and occupied by Germany in 1940. The film includes pastiches of Nazi propaganda newsreels 'so cleverly handled that it might easily seem credible to an uncritical viewer'.[72] *The Battle of Algiers* is perhaps an even more remarkable film: a documentary-drama account of the guerrilla war waged by the Front de la Libération Nationale against the French colonial administration in Algeria between 1954 and 1962. Pontecorvo was commissioned to make the film by the newly independent Algerian government, and it has been seen as an early example of what has since become known as 'Third Cinema' – a 'cinema of liberation' from colonialist oppression.[73] *The Battle of Algiers* consists entirely of reconstructed footage, but so effective was Pontecorvo's pastiche of newsreel film that some audiences apparently mistook it for actuality. A reviewer in the journal *Film Quarterly*, for example, averred that it 'is a film which many viewers felt must be all, or at least partly, newsreel footage; its fidelity to actual historical events was carried past any of the usual goals of fictional re-enactment'.[74] Pontecorvo drew upon the techniques of *Cinéma verité*, such as a hand-held camera and telephoto lens, to create an impression of authenticity that anticipates the 'look' of television coverage of the world's trouble spots: the camera knocked off its axis, the ground-level shots of running feet, the smoke and confusion in the aftermath of a bomb explosion in the kasbah. And, like Brownlow and Mollo, he used a mostly non-professional cast: Jean Martin as tough, hard-nosed French parachute battalion commander, Colonel Mathieu (a character based on General Massu), is the one exception.

Critics were full of praise for the technical and aesthetic effects of Pontecorvo's film, with the notable exception of one Nancy Ellen Dowd, who, in contrast to other commentators, felt that the claims of authenticity made for *The Battle of Algiers* were grossly exaggerated. In her view it was nothing more than a 'collection of romanesque clichés' and a thoroughly 'self-indulgent film'. The film did not come close to any sort of reality, or so she contended, because 'reality is experienced'. This is essentially the same criticism that would later be levelled against *Saving Private Ryan*: that its much-lauded realism was merely a set of representational conventions. 'Film', Dowd averred, 'has provided, or perhaps made obvious, new, more elusive dimensions to the word "representation", and these do not include imitation, reflection, likeness, facsimile.'[75] While her underlying point is undeniably correct – all film involves a degree of artifice and can never be an entirely unmediated reflection of reality – her assessment of the film as clichéd and self-indulgent was not representative of the critical consensus, which regarded it as a powerful and original piece of work.

The reception of *The Battle of Algiers* in the United States was undoubtedly influenced by the growing opposition to the Vietnam War. It was not merely that the French experience in Algeria bore uncomfortable parallels to American involvement in Vietnam (First World military power adopting controversial tactics against a Third World insurgency), but also that, for the first time, images of war were being beamed directly into American living rooms through television. The US release of *The Battle of Algiers* coincided with the Tet Offensive in early 1968. The most notorious image of the time, captured by television cameras as well as stills photographers, was the shooting in the head of a Vietcong prisoner by Colonel Nguyen Ngoc Loan of the South Vietnamese police. This is one of the images credited with turning public opinion against the war; and, while this may be an exaggeration, as opinion polls show that disillusion was mounting before Tet, there is one point that can be made with certainty: of all images of war this particular one is incontestably authentic.

towards an aesthetics of war

It was during the Second World War that the representational conventions of the modern war film emerged. The combat movie became a major genre in the cinemas of the participants, as film-makers sought to legitimate their country's role in the war at the same time as providing the action and spectacle that cinema-going publics demanded. All the major combatants – the United States, Britain, the Soviet Union, Germany, Italy, Japan – produced patriotic war films for propaganda purposes. It would be fair to say that early wartime films, in particular, often reveal an uneasy tension between melodrama and realism. Films such as Germany's *Squadron Leader Lutzow* (*Kampfgeschwader Lutzow*, 1941) and Britain's *Ships With Wings* (1941), for example, are highly fictionalized treatments of aerial combat, having full recourse to melodramatic conventions and studio-bound heroics, interspersed with actuality footage in an attempt to invest the films with a sense of authenticity. The British film was derided by progressive critics because 'the propaganda line of the film would be more appropriate to a Ruritanian campaign than to the Second World War'.[76] The conventional interpretation of the Second World War combat movie is to see it in terms of a gradual convergence between the studio narrative film on the one hand and the style of the documentary film on the other – a process that came to be dubbed the 'wartime wedding'.[77] It was this process that defined both the narrative conventions and the aesthetics of the war film for the next two decades.

Jeanine Basinger argues that in American cinema, for example, the conventions of the combat movie had taken shape by 1943 in films such as *Bataan*, *Guadalcanal Diary*, *Sahara* and *Air Force*. These were films that focused on the combat environment, generally through the device of a unit (platoon, aircrew, etc.) engaged on a particular objective and comprising a diversity of social and ethnic types whose comradeship reflects a sense of national unity. These films were also notable for their psychological realism and authentic representation of military life in contrast to the melodramatic heroics of earlier (pre-1943) films such as *Dive Bomber* or *A Yank in the RAF*. A second wave of films in 1944–5 – *They Were Expendable*, *The Story of GI Joe*, *Objective: Burma!*, *A Walk in the Sun* – 'reflect a realism that is still based on the war itself, but that has taken on an increasingly distanced presentation'.[78] It is in these later wartime films, Basinger contends, that the start of a process of mythologization about the war – a process that culminated with *Saving Private Ryan* – can be detected. The British critic Roger Manvell, similarly, identified 1942 as the year when 'the "war story" with a patriotic slant began to give way to the "war documentary", which derived the action and to a greater extent the characterization from real events and real people'.[79] The crucial transitional film in this process was *In Which We Serve* (1942), Noël Coward's patriotic tribute to the Royal Navy, followed by such documentary-style features as *One of Our Aircraft is Missing*, *We Dive at Dawn*, *Nine Men*, *San Demetrio–London* and *The Way Ahead*.

In the context of the critical culture of the 1940s these films were just as realistic as *Saving Private Ryan*. Indeed, it is instructive to note how the critical reception of the combat movie during the war used much the same vocabulary as the response to the Spielberg film. We can take the reviews of Bosley Crowther, senior film critic of the *New York Times* from 1940, as a barometer of middle-brow tastes. He thought that *Wake Island*, for example, was notable for its 'harsh and bitter detail' and was 'a realistic picture about heroes who do not pose as such'.[80] *Bataan* was 'a picture about war in true and ugly detail'.[81] *Guadalcanal Diary* was 'crammed with heroic action of the grimmest sort'.[82] *Objective: Burma!* 'achieved a startling degree of realism . . . the whole picture has a strong documentary quality'.[83] *Pride of the Marines* was 'visually re-created in a masterfully authentic style'.[84] *They Were Expendable* demonstrated 'complete authenticity' in its representation of the Pacific war.[85] And *The Story of GI Joe* 'has all the integrity and the uncompromising realism of those other great pictorial documents of the Second World War, *The True Glory*, *Desert Victory* and *The Battle of San Pietro*'.[86] Realism continued to be the criterion on which combat films were judged after the end of the war itself. Thus *Sands of Iwo Jima* was a film of 'savage realism';[87] *Battleground* was 'witheringly authentic';[88] *Twelve O'Clock High* exhibited 'rugged realism and punch';[89] *Halls of Montezuma* was a 'remarkably real and agonizing demonstration of the horribleness of war';[90] and *Attack!* was 'a ruthlessly realistic drama'.[91] In Britain, similarly, the (anonymous) film columns of *The Times* detected a new realism in British war films. In *The Next of Kin*, for example, 'the sequences of a raid by our commandos are constructed with considerable realism, and the camera does not gloss over the fact that, in battle, men die violent and horrible deaths'.[92] And in *Nine Men* 'the bayonet fighting at the end has a grimness which would not dare show its nose in any studio-conceived film of warfare'.[93]

A comparison of the combat scenes in *Nine Men* with those of *Saving Private Ryan* shows how perceptions of realism have changed over half a century. *Nine Men* (1943), directed for Ealing Studios by Harry Watt, is a patrol movie focusing on a group of British soldiers who are cut off in the desert and find themselves surrounded by a numerically superior Italian force. It is a taut, spare, economical narrative that, at a mere 68 minutes, is less than half the length of *Saving Private Ryan*. The dramatic climax of *Nine Men*, like *Ryan*, is a last-ditch defensive action to hold a position until relief arrives, with the vastly outnumbered British fighting desperately with their hands and bayonets after they run out of ammunition: Sergeant Watson (played by Jack Lambert), left in charge following the death of the officer, wields a machete during the hand-to-hand combat. Lacking the computer-generated effects available to Spielberg, Watt resorts to the tried-and-tested technique of montage – fast editing and tight close-ups – to create an impression of violent combat. It is a brutal fight: up to half a dozen Italian troops are 'stuck' with a bayonet and two others are strangled or choked with bare hands. Yet there is none of the blood and guts so visible in *Ryan*: the moment of physical penetration is filmed from behind or side-on to the victim and is cut with reaction shots of the faces of the soldiers. This may be physically less realistic than *Ryan*, though it is no less realistic in emotional or psychological terms. It seems perfectly reasonable to assume that wartime audiences did not believe that the act of killing was bloodless just because they saw no blood on the screen: they were exposed to images of death on a regular basis through newsreels and newspapers. Indeed, there is evidence that, the restrictions imposed by a more rigorous censorship regime notwithstanding, film-makers exercised a voluntary restraint for fear of alienating audiences by transgressing acceptable boundaries of decency and taste. One viewer, for example, was moved to protest

> against the showing of dead soldiers on war films. Young and sensitive people are not protected from the sight of these films, and if humanity, culture, morality, and other of the finer human attributes are to survive, these displays of the final result of violence and brutality are not the way to help it.[94]

The critic Ernest Lindgren contended that *Nine Men* 'comes as near to a native style of British film-making as anything which has yet been seen'.[95] Its spare, realistic narrative is representative of a trend in British wartime cinema that was strongly influenced by the documentary school. Watt, for example, was a former documentarist: *Nine Men* was his first studio feature film. British films of the Second World War are notable for their commitment to a type of realism marked by unsensational narratives, plausible situations and believable characterizations of 'ordinary' people reinforced by a sober, restrained visual style bordering on the austere. They are films, like the nation itself, shorn of all fat or excess. The emergence of this style was caused in large measure by the Crown Film Unit, the government's official film unit that produced a cycle of innovatory drama-documentaries about branches of the armed services, using members of the services concerned rather than professional actors. *Target for Tonight*, also directed by Watt, was the first in 1941, followed over the next three years by *Coastal Command*, *Close Quarters*, *Fires Were Started* and *Western Approaches*. Eric Rhode avers that *Target for Tonight*

> now seems as evocative of its period as an ugly, narrow-armed utility chair. The bleakness of its aerodrome setting and the awkwardness of its editing and camera placements capture the austerity of the period with a zeal so puritanical that it begins to assume the conviction of a style.[96]

The Times, once again, documents the extent to which this style became the norm. The quality that it most admired was understatement. Thus *Target for Tonight* 'realises the emphasis of under-statement'.[97] *Coastal Command* 'appears to proceed to an unflurried rhythm ... and the humour of understatement running through the dialogue fits into it very entertainingly'.[98] And *Close Quarters* 'was made by the Crown Film Unit, which is another way of saying that it states an heroic case without indulging in heroics and presents the men through the plain, objective mirror of reporting rather than the distorting lens of cinematic fiction'.[99] *Western Approaches* – shot in desaturated Technicolor – had 'the immense advantage of being both authentic and austere'.[100] That the documentary style had crossed over into the mainstream by the middle of the war is evident in the review of the fictional feature

We Dive at Dawn, which averred that

> the best British films have been those which have not
> concerned themselves with the Gestapo and improbable
> adventures in occupied countries but have blended the
> discipline of the documentary with a minimum amount
> of the story-teller's licence and have gone about show-
> ing how normal men react to the normal strains and
> stresses of war.[101]

The 'wartime wedding' persisted into the post-war period. In
1955 *The Times* could claim, with some justification, that *The
Dam Busters* represented the fulfilment of a trend in British
cinema:

> All air war films up to this one have been, as it were,
> working out the fiction-documentary formula, which is
> particularly our own, in the consciousness that further
> possibilities still existed: with *The Dam Busters* it would
> seem that the last word has been said. Here is a full state-
> ment, final and complete.[102]

The sober, understated war film, epitomized by *The Dam
Busters*, is now so indelibly associated with British cinema that it
has come to represent, almost, a national school. It later became
fashionable to deride such films for their stiff-upper-lipped characterizations and for their apparent repression of emotion,
though, as Andy Medhurst has suggested, they are perhaps better

The Dam Busters
(Michael Anderson,
1954).

understood 'as films about repression, rather than as hopelessly repressed films'.[103] This is exemplified by a scene in *The Dam Busters* where the protagonist, Wing Commander Gibson (Richard Todd), preparing for the dangerous raid on the Ruhr dams, has just been informed that his dog has been run over and killed: Gibson is visibly holding back his tears, controlling his grief in order not to be diverted from the mission. It is a scene that, today, lends itself easily to parody, but in the context of the time it was a psychologically realistic expression of the attitude and behaviour of men like Gibson.

British cinema was not the only one where the documentary-realist aesthetic became the dominant mode of expression during and after the Second World War. The impact of the Italian Neo-realist school cannot be overestimated: this was probably the most influential stylistic movement in the history of the medium. Neo-realism is conventionally seen as a response to the social and political dislocation in Italy following the war, though precursors of Neo-realism have been detected in wartime films such as Luchino Visconti's psychological thriller *Obsession* (*Ossessione*, 1943) and Roberto Rossellini's naval war drama *The White Ship* (*La nave bianca*, 1941). Of the canonical Neo-realist films, only Rossellini's *Rome, Open City* (*Roma, città aperta*, 1945) and *Paisà* (1946) are strictly about the experiences of war. Bazin believed 'that the success of *Roma, città aperta* . . . was inseparable from a special conjunction of historical circumstances that took its meaning from the Liberation'.[104] The film is a documentary-drama account of events between the German occupation of Rome in September 1943 and the Allied liberation of the city in June 1944: it was shot mostly on location in the war-ravaged streets and tenements, using whatever equipment and film stock were available. Consequently, the film possesses a rough, raw-edged austerity of style that critics were quick to dub 'realist' when it was shown abroad.

Bazin argued that the emergence of the new realism in film during the 1940s derived from 'the growth of certain national schools, in particular the dazzling display of the Italian cinema and of a native English cinema freed from the influence of Hollywood'.[105] The realist aesthetic was also adopted as the preferred mode of expression in other national cinemas that all had their different war stories to tell after 1945. The influence of Neo-realism is evident in the *Trümmerfilme* ('rubble films') made in Germany in the mid-1940s, though in contrast to 'pure' Neo-realism these films, such as *The Murderers Are Among Us* (*Die Mörder sind unter uns*, 1946) and *Marriage in the Shadows* (*Ehe im Schatten*, 1947), also harked back to the expressionist visual style of German films of the 1920s, especially in their lighting effects and artfully composed shots of rubble-strewn landscapes. Early post-war French cinema also embraced the documentary-drama mode in resistance films such as *The Battle of the Rails* (*La bataille du rail*, 1945). The British critic Richard Winnington described this film as

> a condensation of all Railway Resistance during [the] Occupation put into superlative rhythmic documentary shape by René Clement. There is no lingering, no declaiming, no attempt to hide a certain volatile small boy's enjoyment of sabotage . . . there is a natural, unescapable dramatic tension and speed and perfect unostentatious playing by everybody.[106]

And when the cinema of the German Federal Republic once again felt able to explore the subject of the Second World War in the 1950s it did so in a style that consciously avoided any visual excess (too reminiscent of the 'Nazi aesthetic' of Third Reich cinema) and instead adhered to the semi-documentary mode. *The Jackboot Mutiny* (*Der 20. Juli*, 1955) and *Stalingrad* (1958), for example, both employ authenticating devices such as a didactic voice-over commentary and the insertion of actuality footage in order to establish their documentary credentials.

Why did the documentary-realist aesthetic become the dominant mode for the visual and narrative representation of war during the 1940s and '50s? There are a number of likely explanations. One, certainly, is economic: the relative poverty of European film industries in comparison to Hollywood encouraged an economical method of film-making that was more suited to low-key production values, location shooting and visual authenticity. Allied to this was the cultural and political imperative for German and Italian film-makers, especially, to differentiate post-war films from the elaborate spectacles that had characterized the cinemas of those nations during the Fascist era. A common trait of most European national cinemas in the 1950s, furthermore, was the telling of 'true' stories of incidents and individuals from the recent war. These films naturally inclined to a realist treatment: indeed, the films often assert their own authenticity through on-screen captions declaring their basis in 'fact'.

There is a more profound psychological explanation, moreover, in that the Second World War was a very recent memory that most cinema audiences, at least until the late 1950s, would have experienced at first hand. There is evidence to suggest that, at least in those territories where American films were shown, European audiences preferred their home-grown war stories to the guts-and-glory version offered by Hollywood. And, finally, there is the simple fact that after so long a set of representational conventions became standardized. It was for this reason that the director Michael Anderson chose to shoot *The Dam Busters* in black-and-white and standard aspect ratio, for example, at a time when colour and widescreen were real possibilities.[107] And, at a time in the early 1960s when most epics and war films were made in colour (*El Cid*, *Lawrence of Arabia*, *The Great Escape*, *Zulu*), Zanuck chose to make *The Longest Day* in monochrome in order to achieve the authenticity he desired. Bosley Crowther observed that 'the picture has been photographed in black-and-white to give a virtual newsreel authenticity to the realistic battle scenes . . . The total effect of the picture is that of a huge documentary report.'[108]

Elsewhere, however, there is evidence of a more 'poetic' treatment of war that shifts away from austere realism. This tendency is most apparent in the cinemas of Eastern Europe during the 'Thaw' following the death of Stalin in 1953, when the decline of strict adherence to the tenets of Socialist Realism encouraged a younger generation of post-war film-makers to embrace new styles and aesthetics. The films of the Polish director Andrzej Wajda, for example, were acclaimed for their combination of 'stark realism' and 'poetic vision'. His acclaimed war trilogy – *A Generation* (1954), *Kanal* (1956) and *Ashes and Diamonds* (1958) – exhibits an increasing visual stylization that shifted, especially in the second and third films, from realism to expressionism and symbolism. *A Generation* exhibits the visual

A Generation (Andrzej Wajda, 1955).

influence of Neo-realism: it was shot mostly on location in a war-ravaged suburb of Warsaw and the cast, while not amateurs, were new to the screen. *Kanal*, a grimly heroic account of the Warsaw Uprising, is more stylized, using studio sets to represent the sewers in which much of the action takes place and shot in a *chiaroscuro* style filled with pools of darkness and shadow. It is in *Ashes and Diamonds* that Wajda's direction becomes most stylized: a combination of deep-focus shots with expressionist lighting effects and an almost baroque imagery employed for symbolic effect rather than strict narrative coherence. In one scene, for example, Maciek, the protagonist, and barmaid Krystyna shelter from the rain in a bombed-out church where the *mise-en-scène* foregrounds religious symbols (including an upside-down crucifix that dominates the foreground) as a visual counterpoint to the morally ambiguous narrative. The response to the films when they were shown abroad was mixed. In Britain the *Monthly Film Bulletin* liked *A Generation* for 'its simplicity and direct, well-

Ashes and Diamonds (Andrzej Wajda, 1958).

aimed purpose',[109] but was less keen on *Kanal*, marred by 'an over-indulgence in the conventionally cinematic, and a number of gratuitously arty and theatrical touches',[110] while *Ashes and Diamonds* seemed to 'suggest a striving after visual expression at the expense of that purity of style found in *A Generation*'.[111] Bosley Crowther, however, was impressed by the 'striking visual images' of *Ashes and Diamonds*, remarking that the 'sharply-etched black-and-white action has the pictorial snap and quality of some of the old Soviet pictures of Pudovkin and Eisenstein'.[112]

The combination of realism and expressionism in Wajda's films also influenced film-makers elsewhere in the Eastern bloc. In the Soviet Union, for example, the late 1940s and early 1950s had seen a cycle of heroic epics about the 'Great Patriotic War' that combined newsreel and reconstructed scenes, including *The*

Battle of Stalingrad and *The Fall of Berlin*. It is evident now that these films are somewhat divorced from historical reality: their aim is to promote a heroic image of Stalin, portraying him as sole architect of the Russian victory.[113] Following Khruschev's 'secret speech' in 1956, however, in which he denounced those films promoting the 'cult of personality' around Stalin, Soviet film-makers were encouraged to look at the war from a fresh perspective. Thus Soviet war films from the later 1950s offered a revisionist narrative that moved away from glorifying the Soviet leadership and placed more of an emphasis on the effects of the war on ordinary Russians. The more humanist narratives of films such as *The Cranes Are Flying* (1957) and *Ballad of a Soldier* (1958) also reveal an increasing level of visual stylization, experimenting with devices such as hand-held cameras and slow-motion effects usually associated with art cinema. *The Cranes Are Flying*, which won the Grand Prize at the Cannes Film Festival, is notable for its optical subjectivity and its use of 'imaginary' sequences that led

The Cranes are Flying (Mikhail Kalatozov, 1957).

Ballad of a Soldier
(Grigori Chukhrai, 1959).

Western critics to claim it as part of a modernist avant-garde. *Ballad of a Soldier* includes an extraordinarily surreal sequence of its protagonist, the young infantryman Alyosha, being pursued across the battlefield by a German Tiger tank in which an over-head crane shot tilts so that the landscape is almost upside down. These films were amongst some of the first Soviet pictures released in the West during the Cold War. Western critics noted their 'lyrical' style. Crowther, for example, remarked that *Ballad of a Soldier* was presented 'in such a swift, poetic way that the tragedy of it is concealed by a gentle lyric quality'.[114]

The 'new cinemas' of Eastern Europe in the early 1960s were characterized by their more ambiguous narratives and what is perhaps best described as their subjective realism (in contrast to the supposedly objective realism of the documentary or the Neo-realist schools). In the German Democratic Republic (GDR), for example, there emerged a distinctive style of film-making characterized by fragmented narratives, self-reflexive narration and crisp black- and-white cinematography. *Five Cartridges* (*Fünf Patronen-Hülsen*, 1960) is set during the Spanish Civil War: its orthodox anti-Fascist narrative is informed, however, by a level of psychological intensity in characterization that permits more fully rounded protagonists, who are not all cast in heroic mould. The film is notable, too, for its expressionist visual style that makes extensive use of extreme close ups. *I Was Nineteen* (*Ich war neunzehn*, 1968) combines documentary techniques (long takes, a hand-held camera) with stylization (extreme close-ups, expressionist imagery), while *The Adventures of Werner Holt* (*Die Abenteuer des Werner Holt*, 1965) employs flashbacks and stream of consciousness as its disillusioned protagonist reflects on his experiences. And in the Soviet Union Andrei Tarkovskii's debut film, *Ivan's Childhood* (1962), was notable for its highly stylized presentation. While the narrative adheres to the conventions of the Soviet war film – Ivan is a teenage boy who joins a partisan unit in order to avenge the death of his parents – it is notable for its juxtaposition of 'real' and 'imaginary' sequences and for its lengthy dialogue-free passages. Tarkovskii contrasts Ivan's real wartime experiences with a counter-narrative in which Ivan enjoys an idyllic childhood. The different worlds are represented visually: while the real landscape is burnt and scarred, shot in a bleak, shadowy, disorienting style, Ivan's imagined other life is pictorially beautiful, shot with bright colours and high-contrast lighting. *Ivan's Childhood* won the Grand Prize at the Venice Film Festival, though at home Tarkovskii fell foul of the authorities for his tendency 'to replace narrative causality with poetic articulations'.[115]

While Eastern bloc war films were offering a more 'poetic' and 'lyrical' image of war – a movement that, however, would be curtailed following changes in the political and artistic culture later in the 1960s – Western cinema was characterized by a shift towards spectacle on a massive scale. This was an uneven process and there are exceptions, such as Richard Lester's caustic anti-war satire *How I Won the War* (1967) and Peter Collinson's low-key character study *The Long Day's Dying* (1968), but the major trend in the West during the 1960s was towards bloated epics in which the austere realism of films of the 1940s and '50s has been replaced by an emphasis on sheer scale and size. The success of *The Longest Day*, in which Zanuck had cast major international stars in the principal roles, spawned a cycle of war epics that restaged the major campaigns of the Second World War, including *Battle of the Bulge* (1965), *Anzio* (1968), *Battle of Britain* (1969), *Tora! Tora! Tora!* (1970), *Midway* (1976) and *A Bridge Too Far* (1977). These films can be seen as part of the trend towards the blockbuster that had begun with the biblical epics of the 1950s and gained momentum in the 1960s as the film industry sought to address the decline in cinema attendances whilst taking advantage of international co-production arrangements. The films shift attention away from the psychological realism of wartime and immediate post-war combat movies and focus instead on the noisy spectacle of battle in colour and widescreen. The documentary qualities of *The Longest Day*, however, are less in evidence. Crowther attributed this to the time that had passed since the war: the 21 years between *Battle of the Bulge* and the events it depicted

> is a long time for certain types in Hollywood – those who
> are inclined to make movies about historic happenings so

A Bridge Too Far (Richard Attenborough, 1977).

they will be spectacle rather than true – to maintain a sense of reality and, indeed, a sober regard toward a large military engagement that has here the makings for a huge war spectacle.[116]

It would be unfair to describe all these films as inauthentic – *Battle of Britain*, for example, provides a historically accurate account of the tactics and strategy of the campaign from both sides, including the dispute within RAF Fighter Command over the effectiveness of its 'big wings' – but their adherence to the historical record is often compromised by the dramatic exigencies of the genre. The convention of casting major stars (deemed necessary for the box office as production costs escalated and cinema audiences declined) and the trend for 'epic' (in the sense of size and length) treatments detract from dramatic coherence. René Clement's *Is Paris Burning?* (1965), for example, was an attempt to recreate the liberation of Paris in the semi-documentary monochrome style of *The Longest Day*, but became a bloated and

Battle of Britain (Guy Hamilton, 1969).

confusing narrative that failed to match the qualities of the director's *Battle of the Rails*. Crowther found it a 'vague, diffuse account of the liberation of Paris . . . a conglomeration of the evidently real and the obviously fake'.[117] The dramatic problems of casting major stars was again highlighted by Joseph E. Levine's production of *A Bridge Too Far*, based, like *The Longest Day*, on a book by Cornelius Ryan. The screenwriter, William Goldman, recalled that in order for Levine to attract the box-office names he needed for international sales, he had to mould the dramatic material into star parts, which meant omitting certain incidents, including the five Victoria Crosses won during the Battle of Arnhem.[118]

What these films offer in lieu of dramatic coherence is visual spectacle. This is not merely a matter of expensive production values and widescreen pyrotechnics: it is evident too in their aesthetic qualities. It might seem unusual to think of war in terms of aesthetics, but there are precedents in the genres of war painting and photography that provide aestheticized images of the battlefield. Anthony Mann, for example, brought to *The Heroes of*

Telemark (1965) the eye for landscape cinematography that had distinguished his acclaimed westerns during the 1950s. The film's pictorialism divided critics. Crowther found it 'immaculate and scenically beautiful . . . It has some of the finest winter scenery and some of the most beautiful shots of skiing that we've seen in a fictional color film.'[119] David Wilson in the *Monthly Film Bulletin*, however, felt that Mann's pictorialism worked against a film that 'leaves one too often with the impression of watching a series of art calendar photographs. The déecor is so consistently magnificent that the film has about it an air of unreality.'[120] *Battle of Britain* suffers dramatically from its thin characterizations and from the difficulty that one actor in a pilot's mask looks much like another, but its scenes of aerial combat 'are certainly spectacularly staged and shot, particularly in the long sequence towards the end when the engine noises and the rattle of guns are cut out and what survives of William Walton's original score accompanies a visually engrossing aerial ballet'.[121] The climactic sequence of the film is choreographed with a level of aesthetic precision that comes close to replicating the stylized imagery of war artists such as Paul Nash: the criss-crossing aircraft and wispy vapour trails recreate the surreal topography of the battle fought in the skies above southern England in the summer of 1940. And *A Bridge Too Far*, which marked the last of the cycle of international war epics, was 'enlivened by the occasional touch of the celluloid poetry of warfare (elegant tank tracks and the uncoiling glider lines)'.[122]

That film-makers have used the camera to aestheticize the battlefield has been evident since the early days when actuality footage on its own was deemed insufficiently interesting for audiences. Haggith observes that 'the battlefield in feature films has a composition and artistic quality which is theatrical and intrinsically pleasing'.[123] In particular, film imposes a structure and order onto the battlefield in order to make it comprehensible for spectators. The modern battlefield is fundamentally unsuitable to the needs of the cinematographer: no longer do armies assemble in neat linear formations or attack in carefully choreographed sequences. Yet this is the impression given in filmed battle sequences. The nearest comparison is to the televising of a football match: in order to maintain continuity the action is shot from one side of the pitch so that each team always attacks in the same direction. This is as true of actuality film as it is of the feature film. Service cameramen were trained to shoot their footage so that it would be easy to edit into a sequence. They were taught the basic principles of feature-film narration by shooting action in such a way that they did not cross the imaginary 180-degree line. Lieutenant-Commander John W. McLain, a cameraman with the us Marine Corps in the Pacific, claimed that he was informed of the invasion plan for Iwo Jima so that he could plan how to film it. He claimed that 'photographers were instructed to shoot American action right to left, and enemy action left to right, thus enabling the public to get a good perspective of the action from the screen and also to help the film cutters do a better job'.[124]

The imposition of a structure onto the battlefield has been a consistent feature of film from the Civil War episodes of D. W. Griffith's *The Birth of a Nation* (1915) to the mythical landscapes of Helm's Deep or the Pelennor Fields in the fantasy epics *The*

Henry v (Laurence Olivier, 1944).

Lord of the Rings: The Two Towers (2002) and *The Lord of the Rings: The Return of the King* (2003). There are certain established conventions: either the opposing armies will clash in an open space or one side will defend a fortress while the other lays siege to it. The principles of continuity editing are maintained, however, so that armies attack in one direction and retreat in the other. This principle is most brilliantly employed in Laurence Olivier's film of *Henry V* (1944). *Henry V* was a patriotic, triumphalist, Technicolor epic that set out to draw explicit historical parallels with inspiring deeds from the past. It shows Britain taking the offensive against a mighty foe: released in the autumn of 1944, following the Normandy landings and the Battle of Arnhem, *Henry V* declared its propagandist credentials through its dedication 'to the Commandos and Airborne Troops of Great Britain – the spirit of whose ancestors it has humbly been attempted to recapture in some ensuing scenes'. The highlight of the film, formally and structurally, is the Battle of Agincourt, where the heavily outnumbered English army bests the mighty

French knights. This action set piece is far from being an authentic reconstruction of a medieval battlefield, but it is one of the outstanding filmic spectacles of war.

The Agincourt sequence is formally structured around planes of movement and stasis: the mounted French knights charge from left to right towards the English lines, where archers wait with their bows poised before unleashing their deadly volley. The most famous shot is a long tracking shot as the knights, starting at a walk, break into a canter and then a full charge. While commentators at the time and since have averred that Olivier based Agincourt on the Battle on the Ice in Sergei Eisenstein's *Alexander Nevsky* (1938) – an equally *bravura* set piece notable for the depth of its *mise-en-scène* – Olivier maintained that he was adhering to an older formal principle: 'The importance to me of this probably unimportant point lies in an English left to right movement rule, and a French right to left movement rule which I had adopted in the film in order really to promote a theory that I have always had (though probably not the first to have it) regarding the rules of the English stage.'[125] In fact, there are significant differences between *Alexander Nevsky*, which, in line with Eisenstein's theory of a 'montage of attractions' breaks the 180-degree rule in its conflicting angles and opposing movements, and *Henry V*, which preserves the formal unities and thus imposes a clearer sense of structure onto the order of battle.

There are examples where film-makers have attempted to dramatize the confusion of battle. Tony Richardson's version of *The Charge of the Light Brigade* (1968), for example, is at pains to show the Battle of Balaclava as a military blunder rather than a heroic spectacle. The sequences leading up to the battle demonstrate the confused orders that led to the Light Brigade charging into the wrong valley: the topography of the battlefield is visible to the staff officers directing the battle from a hilltop but not to those at the head of the brigade itself. A misleading order is conveyed to the Light Brigade, who proceed to attack the main Russian battery in the north valley rather than recapture some British guns seized in the south valley. The charge itself lacks a clear formal structure – a deliberate decision by Richardson in order to demonstrate the chaos of battle – but the result makes it confusing for the spectator. Critics seized upon this point in their reviews; they complained that it 'leaves us almost as muddled as the men below as to what went on' and that it was 'a well-nigh intolerable mess'.[126]

This treatment, however, remains the exception rather than the rule. Film-makers prefer to represent their celluloid campaigns according to the principles of cinema rather than the messy realities of battle. This even extends to the explanation of military strategy, which in *A Bridge Too Far* is explained through a filmic metaphor. General Horrocks (Edward Fox) briefs his officers thus:

> I like to think of this as one of those American Western films. The paratroops, lacking substantial equipment, always short of food – these are the besieged homesteaders. The Germans, well naturally they're the bad guys. And Thirty Corps – we, my friends, are the cavalry on the way to the rescue.

There are, indeed, some significant points of comparison between the war film and the western, not least in the fact that so many of the major directors of westerns have also made accomplished war films: John Ford (*The Battle of Midway*, *They Were Expendable*), Raoul Walsh (*Objective: Burma!*), John Sturges (*The Great Escape*), Anthony Mann (*The Heroes of Telemark*) and Sam Peckinpah (*Cross of Iron*).

A Bridge Too Far was made at sufficient remove from the events it depicted to offer a detached perspective that might even be described as anti-war. Yet even explicitly anti-war films tend to aestheticize the subject. The titles of *The Birth of a Nation* asserted that 'in this work we have conveyed to the mind the ravages of war to the end that war may be held in abhorrence'. Yet at the same time the film was promoted as a spectacular attraction in which audiences were invited to share the thrill and excitement. Joseph Henabery, who appeared in the film as Abraham Lincoln and later became an assistant director

Apocalypse Now (Francis Ford Coppola, 1979).

for Griffith's *Intolerance*, remarked: 'you enjoyed it all the more because you became involved in the battle. You weren't just a by-stander, you were emotionally involved.'[127] The tension in film between representing the unpleasant reality of war and the sensual excitement of combat is nowhere better demonstrated than in Francis Ford Coppola's Vietnam epic *Apocalypse Now* (1979), in which the most memorable sequence is the bombard-ment of a Vietnamese village by a squadron of American heli-copters. Coppola achieves beautifully composed images of the helicopters in formation against an orange sky, while the sound-track resonates to the strains of Wagner's *Ride of the Valkyries* played at volume by the attacking troops ('My men love it. It scares the hell out of the gooks'). Vincent Canby in the *New York Times* described it as 'a display of barbarism that is simul-taneously lyrical and terrifying'.[128] It has been alleged that during the invasion of Grenada in 1983 some detachments of US

Marines went ashore playing Wagner in imitation of Robert Duvall's Colonel Kilgore.[129] Here is evidence of war being conducted according to its filmic representation, and eloquent testimony of the power of cinema to influence, even to determine, perceptions of combat.

virtual war

Over the last two decades the distinction between war as it is experienced and war as it is represented in visual culture has become so blurred that a new vocabulary has emerged in the theoretical discourse around the subject. The terms now bandied about – 'virtual war', 'cyber war', 'net-war', 'postmodern war', 'spectator-sport war' – indicate an epistemological shift in the way in which war is understood. Arising from the media coverage of the first Gulf War of 1991 and of NATO's aerial campaign over Kosovo in 1999, and lent intellectual weight by theorists such as Jean Baudrillard, the concept of 'virtual war' refers to changes both in the conduct of modern warfare and the media's representation of it.

The nature of warfare in the late twentieth and early twenty-first centuries is of a very different order from the two World Wars. Since the end of the Cold War the prospect of a global war between rival geopolitical power blocs involving nuclear weapons has become less likely. Post-1989 armed conflict has consisted of so-called limited wars taking place in clearly defined theatres with relatively straightforward strategic objectives, rather than 'total war' involving the complete economic and ideological mobilization of states. In the first Gulf War – and, prior to that, the Falklands War of 1982 – the conflict involved the expulsion of an aggressive military power from territory it had invaded. In other instances, such as Somalia and Kosovo, war takes the form of 'intervention' under the authority of the United Nations to prevent humanitarian catastrophe caused by racial genocide. The strategic objectives of wars against the Taliban regime in Afghanistan in 2001 and against Iraq in 2003 were, on both occasions, regime change; despite the likelihood of prolonged military deployment in these regions, however, the wars themselves remain 'limited' in comparison to the World Wars, Korea or Vietnam.

The idea of limited war also imposes certain limitations on the conduct of war, especially the extent of legitimate force. Jeremy Black has argued that the prosecution of modern war is inhibited by cultural factors: on the one hand the desire not to sustain heavy casualties and, on the other, the desire not to inflict unnecessary casualties on the enemy, especially on civilians caught in the crossfire.[130] From an American perspective, especially, the legacy of Vietnam haunts the military: it is widely (if inaccurately) believed that television images of US servicemen in 'body bags' and pictures of maimed Vietnamese children were instrumental in turning public opinion against the war. Thus it is that the 'management' of media reporting by the military now deliberately creates a distance from the real experience of war. One tactic is the resort to an obtuse military jargon that employs phrases such as 'material degradation' (bombardment) and 'collateral damage' (a euphemism for civilian casualties). Another tactic is the emphasis on so-called smart weapons such as laser-guided bombs and cruise missiles that are able to 'take out' their targets with pinpoint accuracy. No matter that the claims made for the accuracy of such weapons are invariably exaggerated or that most ordnance used in the Gulf and Iraq wars was of the conventional 'dumb' variety: there is an overriding imperative on the part of military authorities to demonstrate that modern warfare is a 'clean' and 'surgical' enterprise conducted with absolute precision in order to minimize casualties.

The impression of clean, casualty-free warfare is further enhanced by the media, and particularly by television. Television provides sanitized images of war in two forms. On the one hand it plays, and replays, those (selective) video images provided by the military authorities. Such images never show people: the targets are always 'infrastructures' (bridges, railways, buildings) or 'hardware' (tanks, vehicles, ordnance). Then, when it has exhausted its library of stock footage, television creates its own images through tactical diagrams, maps and increasingly sophisticated simulations that use computer-generated imaging to recreate the battlefield environment. CNN (Cable News Network) came of age during the Gulf War and its rolling 24-hour news coverage gave the impression of events unfolding in 'real time'. To this extent war has become just another form of entertainment, competing with sporting contests and royal occasions as a televised 'event'. This is what Michael Ignatieff means when he writes that war has become form of a spectator sport: television viewers of NATO's aerial campaign over Kosovo 'were mobilized, not as combatants but as spectators. The war was a spectacle: it aroused emotions in the intense but shallow way that sports do.'[131]

It has been argued that images of 'virtual war' have now become so indistinguishable from those of 'real war' that the distinction between the two has become meaningless. It was this phenomenon that led Baudrillard to his infamous statement that 'The Gulf War Did Not Take Place'. This remark has sometimes been wilfully misread to suggest that Baudrillard was denying the fact of the Gulf War in the same way that some conspiracy theorists deny the fact of the Moon landings and insist that they were an elaborate deception by NASA. Rather, what Baudrillard meant was that we should consider the extent to which images of the 'real' war provided by the Pentagon had merged with the 'virtual' war of simulation. The television coverage of the Gulf War seemed an ideal illustration of the post-structuralist notion that we experience the world not through actuality but through its representation. To this extent the Gulf represented a new type of warfare that, or so Baudrillard claimed,

> wreaks its havoc at another level by trickery, hyperreality, simulcra, by the entire mental strategy of deterrence which is played out in the facts and in the images, in the anticipation of the real by the virtual, of the event by virtual time, and in the inexorable confusion of the two.[132]

Baudrillard argued that the Gulf War had been scripted – and won – in advance: that the outcome was predicted by its imagining. It is an impressionistic argument in the extreme and has certainly been accorded more intellectual weight than it properly deserves. That said, however, the work of other scholars, more empirically focused and theoretically rigorous, has developed the idea of 'virtual war' beyond the Dadaist anti-prediction jokes of the early 1990s. James Der Derian, for example, suggests that collusion between the military and media industries has led to the emergence of something he calls MIMENET (the military-industrial-media-entertainment network). He points to the way in which military planning for future conflicts has had recourse to simulations graphically engineered with the assistance of the Disney Corporation. Not only does this have the effect of turning war into virtual reality – rather like a computer game or a role-playing exercise – but it also suggests that strategists are now more preoccupied with the mediated projection of war than with actually fighting it.[133]

I would contend, however, that rather than signifying an entirely new departure in the visual realization of war, the debate over 'virtual war' simply rehearses issues that have been present since early cinematographers first took their cameras into the field. It is the absence of actuality footage that necessitates reconstruction and simulation: to this extent the close management of the media by the military is really no different from the situation before 1916 when all sides were reluctant to allow cameramen access to the front. That images of war have always been highly mediated was exemplified by combat documentaries like *The Battle of the Somme* and *Desert Victory*, which, as we have seen, had recourse to reconstruction. Nor is the 'Disneyfication' of war an entirely new phenomenon. In 1943, for example, Disney had produced an animated feature film based on Major Alexander de Seversky's controversial book *Victory Through Air Power*, which had argued for the importance of strategic bombing in the war against Germany and Japan. The climax of the film depicts an American eagle bombing a Japanese octopus until it loses its grip on the Pacific. The film industry has a long history of producing training and propaganda films for the military: its role in providing simulations of future combat scenarios is merely an extension of that role rather than a new departure.

Moreover, the two foremost characteristics of 'virtual war' – its insistence on 'clean' images of combat and its privileging of optical subjectivity – have always been part of the filmic representation of war. One of the aims of *Target for Tonight*, for example, was to demonstrate the accuracy of Bomber Command in its strategic bombing offensive in contrast to the indiscriminate nature of the Luftwaffe. To this extent it made grossly exaggerated claims for the effects of precision bombing at a time when, in reality, barely a third of British bombers could even find their designated targets at night, let alone actually hit them.[134] It could be argued, indeed, that for all its claims to documentary authenticity, *Target for Tonight* was a precursor of 'virtual war' since it includes simulated shots from the perspective of the enemy that are 'impossible' in a strict documentary sense. The editing of the film 'draws attention to the status of the images as being – while obviously keeping their own referential relationship to a prior world – a part of the telling, not a part of the told'.[135]

The other major characteristic of 'virtual war' is its optical subjectivity: placing the spectator in the position of both observer and participant. The classic example is the infra-red image from the laser-guided bomb gliding inexorably to its target lined up between the cross hairs: an image that was widely used during the Kosovo and Iraq campaigns to demonstrate the accuracy of 'smart' weapons. Yet this image is nothing new and has been part of the cinematic apparatus since the very early days of the medium when 'phantom rides' were a favourite genre of film-makers exploring the potential of camera subjectivity. A phantom ride was a film taken from a camera fixed on the front of a moving vehicle, usually a train, tram or omnibus, which gave the illusion of movement. A similar effect was achieved during the Second World War with operational footage of combat operations shot from cameras fixed to the nose or wings of combat aircraft. It soon became a convention of aerial combat films, both fictional and documentary, to include point-of-view shots through the bombsight and overhead shots of bombs falling into space. One of the earliest examples of this effect is in William Wyler's *The Memphis Belle*, a documentary record of the final combat mission by the first US Air Force B-17 'flying fortress' to complete a 'tour' of 25 operational sorties: the film includes various images – the under-wing shot of the plane's wheels retracting, the shot along the barrel of the machine gun firing at enemy fighters, the shot of the ground through the bombsight – that have since become clichés of the aerial combat film. (Wyler evidently appreciated the aesthetic possibilities of aerial photography: two years later he used shots from the nose of a B-17 during the sequence in *The Best Years of Our Lives* where the three servicemen hitch a ride home.) The point-of-view shot through the bombsight, in particular, is another form of spectacle: the shot always has the effect of drawing attention to itself due to its extreme subjectivity. This insistence on optical subjectivity – what Virilio describes as 'the logistics of perception' – has long been a feature of the war film.[136]

The cultural theory critique of 'virtual war' maintains that the modern media project a sanitized image of war: one that is fought by technology rather than by human beings. And it maintains that the human consequences of war are screened out by an overriding emphasis on technology. This critique seems to me entirely misplaced. For one thing it is simply untrue that media coverage of contemporary conflict omits its human consequences: there are plentiful examples to the contrary in the reporting of the conflicts in Bosnia and Iraq. And in the first Gulf War it was widely held that it was television pictures of the 'highway of death' north of Kuwait City that prompted the US-led coalition to cease hostilities against retreating Iraqi forces, though, as Philip Taylor has demonstrated, a ceasefire had in fact been ordered by President George Bush before the images were broadcast.[137]

Yet even if we accept the notion of 'virtual war' at face value, it needs to be placed in the wider context of a visual culture that is saturated with images of violence and death. Not only has satellite broadcasting made it possible for 'real' war to be recorded and transmitted in 'real' time, but advances in digital special-effects technology have also made it possible to reconstruct the battlefield environment with greater verisimilitude than ever before. At a time when, in the eyes of cultural theorists, we are being prevented from seeing the real thing by the aesthetic of 'virtual war', cinema audiences seem to have an appetite for increasingly realistic representations of violent conflict in films such as *Saving Private Ryan* and *Black Hawk Down* (2002). While these films may be as 'virtual' in their own way as the efforts of MIMENET, their intention is quite different: they attempt not to disguise the nature of war but to show it for what it is. There is an irony, therefore, in the fact that while the coverage of 'real' war is becoming more distant from its subject, the filmic reconstruction of war is becoming ever more realistic in effect. It is a trend, moreover, that is not confined to the West. The South Korean film *Brotherhood* (*Taegukgi*, 2004), for example, was praised for its 'harrowing combat sequences' that drew favourable comparison with *Ryan*.[138] The film opens with a bloody sequence of the battle for the Nakdong River that includes incinerated corpses, dismembered bodies and limbs pierced by bayonets. This imagery might be artificial in a strictly theoretical sense; but a sanitized representation of war it certainly is not.

Yet it is not necessary to resort to expensively staged battlefield pyrotechnics to show the human consequences of war. Michael Winterbottom's film *Welcome to Sarajevo* (1997), for example, inspired by the real-life experiences of an ITN reporter, Michael Nicholson, in 1992, is one of the most humane and sincere studies of the effects of war on those who experience it at first hand. The film follows television journalist Michael Henderson (Stephen Dillane), reporting the siege of Sarajevo during the civil war in Bosnia: frustrated by the impotence of the United Nations in evacuating civilians from the combat zone, he undertakes to rescue an eleven-year-old girl from an orphanage and take her to England where he and his wife adopt her. While the war correspondent as a protagonist is not a new device – previous examples of the genre include *The Year of Living Dangerously* (1982), *The Killing Fields* (1984) and *Salvador* (1986) – what distinguishes *Welcome to Sarajevo* is not so much its story but its style of presentation. Winterbottom adopts a documentary-style *Cinéma verité* technique that uses authentic locations (the film was shot in Sarajevo shortly after the end of the civil war), mixes real and mocked-up news footage, and employs jarring devices such as jump cuts and freeze frames. Its mixture of authenticity and stylization recalls *The Battle of Algiers*, though Winterbottom's film has a more conventional narrative structure as Henderson's effort to rescue the orphaned Emira takes prominence. Some critics felt that the 'feel-good' optimism of the film diminished its agitprop effect, though given the story's basis in fact it is difficult to see how it could have done otherwise. *Sight and Sound* thought it 'epic in its scope and ambitious in its intentions'.[139] It was widely recognized as a technical *tour de force* whose distinguishing characteristic was Winterbottom's 'rigorously restrained camera movement'. 'In virtually every frame,' wrote one commentator, 'the camera functions as an independent, keen, empathic consciousness, moving of its own discerning will around the city and through the anarchical day-to-day nightmare lives of its citizens.'[140]

Welcome to Sarajevo can also be seen as a commentary on the nature of televised war and the aestheticization of violence. It is told from the perspective of those who witness war at first hand

Welcome to Sarajevo (Michael Winterbottom, 1997).

but who are also in the business of reporting it for the media. On one level the film is a critique of the political economy of the modern media industries and the public's fascination with triviality. Thus the journalists are outraged to discover that the lead story on the television news is not the siege of Sarajevo but the divorce of the Duke and Duchess of York. Indeed, Henderson's decision to privilege the story of an orphanage 'in the most dangerous corner of the most dangerous city on earth' is presented initially not as a humanitarian act on his part but as an attempt to find a 'human interest' story that will more easily meet the requirements of the media. Moreover, *Welcome to Sarajevo* is evidently informed by the cultural theory critique of war reporting that was emerging at the time of its production. Thus, on the one hand, in what seems like a direct riposte to Baudrillard and Ignatieff, Henderson's colleague Gregg (James Nesbitt) snorts

contemptuously: 'It's all this news as entertainment bollocks – it's all so patronizing.' On the other hand, however, the film seems to suggest that the reporters themselves have become so desensitized to the scenes of death and destruction they witness that they can relate to the world around them only through mediated images. On several occasions the point of view of the journalists is represented by grainy video images revealing a queasy fascination with the spectacle of dead bodies: it is as if they can look at the carnage only through the camera's lens. Thus even those on the front line 'see' war not as the real thing but through a mediated form of visual representation.

Welcome to Sarajevo is both a deeply humane and a deeply humanistic film. Its main theme is that, even in the midst of the most dreadful circumstances, the actions of one person can make a difference. It therefore endorses the notion of individual agency as emphatically as *Saving Private Ryan*. Unlike *Ryan*, however, *Welcome to Sarajevo* uses its revulsion at the images of conflict to enforce a more overt anti-war message. Henderson describes Sarajevo as being 'like a virus you can't rid of': this idea of war as a disease or plague is a recurring theme of anti-war cinema. In focusing on civilians caught in a conflict zone, furthermore, *Welcome to Sarajevo* is a rare example of a film that explores the effects of war on supposed non-combatants. One of the themes of the combat movie has always been the suggestion that war can be understood properly only by those who have participated in it and that the comradeship of servicemen is a special bond unique to those who have fought in war. This idea is afforded prominence in recent *Ryan*-influenced films such as *Brotherhood* and in the television series *Band of Brothers*. The achievement of a film like *Welcome to Sarajevo*, however, is to bring home the extent to which war does not differentiate between combatant and non-combatant. For those caught in a combat zone, soldier and civilian alike, war is anything but 'virtual'.

2 war as tragedy

total war

'This is WAR! Total horror, everywhere. To recreate the sensual image of war, to convey this to the viewer, especially the young viewer who has never seen war, but plays at war. That's one of the aims of our work.'[1] This quotation from the Soviet director Elem Klimov, referring to his film *Come and See* (*Idi i smotri*, 1985), recalls Steven Spielberg's comment that the aim of *Saving Private Ryan* had been 'to resensitize audiences to how bad it was'. The success of Spielberg's Second World War epic had revived interest in Klimov's earlier film, which, after winning the Gold Prize at the Moscow Film Festival and enjoying a limited 'art house' release in the West, during which it attracted good notices, had since largely disappeared from critical consciousness. Even following its 'rediscovery', *Come and See* is a much less well-known film than *Saving Private Ryan*, though it has an equal if not greater claim to representing war at its most harrowing. There were some critics who, partly reacting against the extravagant claims made for *Saving Private Ryan*, suggested instead that Klimov's film more properly deserved the accolade of 'the war film to end all war films'.[2]

Come and See, based on Alexander Adamovich's book *I Am from the Fiery Village* (1978), was produced to commemorate the fortieth anniversary of what Russian historians still refer to as the Great Patriotic War.[3] Unlike either the didactic propaganda of films like *The Fall of Berlin* or the lyricism of *Ballad of a Soldier*, however, *Come and See* is a stark and uncompromising tale of the war in Belorussia. And in contrast to the classically goal-driven and highly structured narrative of *Saving Private Ryan*, *Come and See* is almost shapeless: it is episodic and picaresque with a loose structure and no real sense of closure. It is told from the point of view of Florian, a boy of about twelve or thirteen, who joins the partisans and witnesses the horrors of war at first hand. Florian initially finds the life of the partisans exciting and admires their leader, Kosach. When the partisans go into action, Florian is left behind to mind the camp with Glasha, a teenage girl who may be Kosach's lover. The camp is bombed, and Florian is temporarily deafened by the explosions. Florian and Glasha, forced to leave the camp by the arrival of German parachutists, make their way to Florian's home, only to find his mother and sisters have been killed. They make an arduous trek through inhospitable marshes where Florian, traumatized by the death of his family, for which he holds himself responsible, nearly drowns Glasha. Eventually they find the new camp of partisans where people from Florian's village are also sheltering, including the horribly burned village elder. Florian and three other partisans are sent to forage for food, but two are killed when they stray into a minefield. Florian and the remaining partisan, Rubezh, steal a cow from a farmer, but Rubezh and the cow are killed in a sudden burst of machine-gun fire. Florian hides his rifle and is taken home by the farmer, who tries to pass the boy off as his son

Come and See (Elem Klimov, 1985).

when a German ss unit arrives to round up the local population. The villagers are herded into a barn, which is set on fire. Florian survives by a sheer fluke: he is caught climbing out of a window, but the laughing, drunken German soldiers do not bother to kill him. Later, in the woods, Florian comes across the remnants of the German unit, which has been ambushed by Kosach's partisans. Florian retrieves his rifle. He finds Glasha, who has been savagely beaten and raped. Florian shoots at a framed portrait of Hitler in the mud. The film ends with Florian running to catch up with the partisans as they head off into the forest.

Come and See is shot in the style of a documentary-drama, using non-professional actors as the villagers and subdued naturalistic colours. Klimov and his cameraman Alexei Rodionov employ widescreen and a Steadicam to create a sense of immediacy: the film is full of extreme close-ups of faces and does not flinch from the unpleasant details of burnt flesh and bloodied corpses. The *mise-en-scène* is fragmentary and disjointed: there are discontinuities between shots as characters appear in close up and then disappear off camera. And there are some jarring edits: a shot of Florian and Rubezh milking the cow in the early light of dawn cuts suddenly to tracer bullets flashing across the night sky. Above all the film is memorable for its harrowing and occasionally surreal imagery: Florian and Glasha showering in the rain, a stork prowling quizzically around the deserted partisan camp, an effigy of Hitler made from a skull, the old woman left lying in her bed in the open air. Klimov employs a range of techniques that draw attention to the camera. The extreme close-up of actors staring into camera is a recurring motif. Perhaps the most memo-

Come and See.

rable of these is a shot of a German officer's pistol held against Florian's head; the officer is posing for a photograph. Elsewhere, in the scene where Florian realizes that his family have been killed, the moment of revelation is marked by a disorienting zoom-in/dolly-out shot (the same effect, to cite a more familiar example, as when the police chief witnesses the second shark attack in *Jaws*). At other points in the film the imagery alone is sufficient to convey the horror: it is the blood trickling down Glasha's legs, for example, that conveys how brutally she has been treated. Klimov is at some pains to make the viewing experience difficult for the spectator. This is particularly evident when Florian is deafened by the bombardment of the partisan camp:

the soundtrack switches from 'white noise' to a blurred cacophony of sounds and words until his hearing returns. There is a similar moment in *Saving Private Ryan* when Captain Miller is disoriented on the beach, but whereas Spielberg maintains the effect for about a minute, Klimov persists with it for the next half-hour of the film.

Come and See made a deep impression on critics when it was shown in the West; the film was reviewed more widely than most foreign-language films. Most critics, such as David Robinson in *The Times*, thought it 'a powerful, accomplished, shocking work'.[4] Alexander Walker averred that 'it has a raw, primitive force that makes you realise how much of our own horror of the last war has been diminished by Hollywood heroics'.[5] For Diane Jacobs in the *Village Voice*, it 'renders excruciatingly fresh the grief and madness of war'.[6] While such comments are similar in tone to the reception of *Saving Private Ryan*, however, the film also provoked different responses. If Spielberg's film was most admired for the 'authenticity' and 'realism' of its combat sequences, the effect of Klimov's film was very different. Here it was the 'nightmare' and 'surreal' elements that attracted comment. Philip French of *The Observer* described it as 'a surreal nightmare'.[7] Mark Le Fanu in *Sight and Sound* felt that it had 'the authentic relentlessness of nightmare'.[8] Other critics tried to explain how it moved beyond conventional notions of reality. The *Times Educational Supplement* thought it 'a work of extraordinary power and imagination . . . If there are moments when it touches on the surreal, this is because the war that it represents distorts reality and disrupts the senses.'[9] Walter Goodman in the *New*

York Times described this simply as 'a sort of unreal realism', a term that perfectly summarizes its unusual qualities.[10] Others still, contrasting the content of the film with its visual style, remarked upon its 'beauty'. 'The horror is interspersed with scenes of almost lyrical beauty', wrote Virginia Dignam in the *Morning Star*.[11] And Virginia Mather in the *Daily Telegraph* described it as 'compelling, harrowing, absurdly beautiful . . . an epic diffused by the lyricism of the photography'.[12] A Russian critic, Rostislav Pospelov, similarly felt that 'the film is stark but somehow pure and bittersweet'.[13]

There were some dissenting voices. Several reviews suggested that the film was too stridently propagandistic in its representation of the Germans as uniformly brutal. A minority of critics also felt alienated by Klimov's film-making technique. The most negative response was from David Denby of *New York* magazine who berated Klimov for his 'slovenliness' and for 'the crudity of this movie', which he likened to 'a succession of brutally sincere "art" assaults, jammed together like the poorly articulated cars of an old freight train'. Denby disliked the discontinuities in editing and the unconventional spatial relationships in the film, remarking that

> if Klimov isn't going to make films more reflective than this one, he can at least straighten out such moment-by-moment details as where two military units, or even two people, are standing or hiding in relation to one another, or how a German battalion that is rampaging over the land can suddenly, in the next sequence, wind up in abject captivity.[14]

This charge was rejected by other critics, however, who recognized that Klimov's technique was deliberately disorienting. 'Technically the film is brilliant and powerful,' declared David Robinson, 'at its best in the early parts where the Nazis remain an unseen but ever-present menace.'[15] And Philip Bereson thought it a 'film of the highest artistry, with technique and sentiment utterly in harmony'.[16]

It will be apparent even from this brief account of the film's reception that *Come and See* is a difficult film to watch and an even more difficult one to categorize. In chapter One I argued that the realism of *Saving Private Ryan* is a mimetic form of realism in so far as the protagonists in the film act and behave in a manner that we find psychologically plausible. The same cannot be said of *Come and See*. While we witness Florian's traumatic experiences, it is almost impossible to read his actions in terms of conventional psychological realism. This is due in part to the remarkable performance of Alexei Kravchenko, whose facial expression remains consistently blank throughout, masking the character's emotional state, and in part to the simple fact that, for Western viewers at least, the events depicted in the film are so distant from our own experiences as to be beyond comprehension. We have no real sense of whether Florian's behaviour, such as burying his head in the mud like an ostrich or beating the ground with his hands, is psychologically plausible. In this context the reading of the film as a nightmare seems an entirely appropriate way of understanding it. Like a nightmare, its vivid imagery leaves a stronger impression than its disjointed narrative.

Yet *Come and See* is more than just, as one critic put it, 'a grim sort of picaresque'.[17] If it is non-realistic in both an aesthetic and a psychological sense, it is, nevertheless, authentic as a dramatic reconstruction of real events. Indeed, the film asserts its authenticity through a closing caption informing us that 628 Belorussian villages were razed to the ground and their inhabitants slaughtered. Klimov averred that 'memories of the war are still alive and will never die. That is why every Soviet director should shoot his own film about the war.'[18] To this extent *Come and See* represents a mythologization of the historical experience of the war in Belorussia just as surely as *Saving Private Ryan* does for the Americans in Normandy. At the same time, however, *Come and See* departs from the official Soviet history of the war in several important respects. Thus, while the Nazis are represented in ideologically correct terms as a swarm who rape Russia – both literally and figuratively – the partisans here are decidedly unheroic: they steal from the local population and are absent when the civilians are being massacred. The central protagonist, moreover, is hapless and passive, always reacting to events rather than instigating them. Florian has no apparent ideological or political beliefs: he joins the partisans for the adventure their lifestyle seems to offer ('Just like a summer camp for kids' one partisan tells the boy's mother) and stays with them so he can avenge the massacre of his family. All films are informed by and respond to the cultural and political circumstances of the time at which they made: to this extent Denise Youngblood suggests that 'the pervasive pessimism of *Come and See* easily may be seen as a cinematic reflection of the Soviet public's morale near the end of the regime'.[19]

That said, however, *Come and See* remains perhaps the most powerful representation of the conflict that has more recently been termed the 'war of the century': the brutal war of annihilation fought between Nazi Germany and the Soviet Union.[20] It is only quite recently, and due largely to works of popular history such as Antony Beevor's *Stalingrad* (1998), that the full horrors of the war on the Eastern Front have been brought to the attention of Western publics brought up on a diet of narratives that, during the Cold War, marginalized the role of the Soviet Union in defeating the Nazi war machine. *Come and See* is not a conventional war film about battles between armies; it focuses instead on the effects of war on the civilian population that suffered during the German invasion. The events in the film are a distillation of actual historical experiences. The German attack on the Soviet Union in 1941 was marked by an unprecedented level of brutality and indiscriminate killing as the invaders interpreted very loosely the notorious 'special military measures' for dealing with 'Bolsheviks, agitators, guerrillas, saboteurs and Jews'. It was not only the *Einsatzkommando* ('special commando units') who were involved in anti-partisan operations and reprisals: *Come and See* is probably historically accurate in suggesting that soldiers of the Wehrmacht participated in carrying out atrocities alongside the Waffen ss.

Klimov's equivalent to Spielberg's Omaha Beach sequence is the Perekhody massacre – it occupies a similar amount of screen time – which even twenty years later could still be described as 'one of the most appalling – in the sense of causing extreme dismay – sequences in all cinema'.[21] The sequence is remarkable not only for its documentary-like quality, but also for the sense of casualness that attends the massacre. An *Einsatzkommando* arrives in the village and the troops accept food and drink from the villagers. The villagers are told to assemble outside with their identification, ostensibly for transportation to Germany, though a dead body being paraded on a motorcycle sidecar with a placard declaring 'I insulted a German soldier' is an ominous portent of what is to come. The villagers are herded into a large barn, surrounded by a cordon of German soldiers who are jeering and drinking vodka. Martial music is blaring from loudspeakers. Soldiers toss stick grenades through the windows of the barn while others pour petrol over the wooden walls. Florian clambers out of a window and is made to watch as the barn burns and soldiers shoot casually into the flames. A girl who has escaped the carnage is dragged by her hair across the ground and bundled screaming into the back of a truck full of soldiers. Florian is dragged onto his knees by a German officer, who poses for a photograph with his pistol pressed against the boy's head before simply walking off and leaving him. The Germans depart as the barn burns, wheeling out an old woman lying in her bed and leaving her in the middle of a field. It is a disturbing yet oddly gripping sequence that exerts a very different effect on the spectator from *Saving Private Ryan*. It is unlikely that any critic could compare the Perekhody sequence to a video game or a theme-park ride: there is none of the exhilaration that accompanies Spielberg's film. Instead, the spectator, like Florian, is forced into the position of a horrified witness to an atrocity that unfolds relentlessly before our eyes. It is not so much spectacle as anti-spectacle:

Come and See.

there is no pleasure to be had, but rather a discomforting sense of voyeurism as we watch the horrific acts. We might even compare Klimov's technique to counter-cinema: its intent seems to be to discomfort the spectator and produce a sense of estrangement and 'un-pleasure'.[22]

It is towards the end of the film, however, that Klimov seems to embrace avant-garde practices. As Florian retrieves his rifle and shoots at a framed picture of Hitler left behind by the Germans, the film cuts between shots of Florian and archive newsreel footage of Hitler and the Nazis. Any sense that this is a device to anchor the film in historical reality, however, is contradicted by the fact that the newsreel footage is running backwards. The archive film therefore takes us back through the events of the war, the 1930s, the Nazi accession to power, the Weimar period, the First World War, and finally to a shot of baby Hitler sitting on his mother's knee. At this point Florian stops shooting and turns his back on the camera. It is an extraordinary sequence that defies critical interpretation. Does the reversed footage suggest a desire to reverse history and thus prevent the terror that has been

inflicted on the innocents of Belorussia? If so, then why does Florian not shoot at baby Hitler, who is clearly being presented as the cause of the terror? Or is Klimov implying some sort of link between Florian and the Nazi dictator? Throughout the film we have seen Florian's features age to the extent that by the end he is prematurely grey-haired and his face is craggy and lined. The *Guardian* critic Derek Malcolm, for example, understood the sequence to mean that 'the innocence of childhood is always likely to be corrupted'.[23] Alternatively, it might be argued that the inclusion of this blatantly non-naturalistic sequence near the end of the film has the effect of questioning the nature of historical authenticity. If the archive footage (conventionally understood as a filmic shorthand for authenticity) is open to manipulation then so too is the historical record. The effect, intentionally or otherwise, therefore might be to undermine the claim for authenticity made by Klimov's film – a characteristic device of counter-cinema that draws attention to the artifice of the medium.

These points are speculative; Klimov does not seem to have offered any explanation for the sequence. What can be asserted, unequivocally, is that *Come and See* remains a vivid, harrowing representation of the brutal extremes of genocidal war. In contrast, the violence of many Hollywood war movies, including *Saving Private Ryan* and *Apocalypse Now*, seems highly sanitized. It is the random and indiscriminate nature of the violence in *Come and See* that is most disturbing: that Florian survives the holocaust is due to sheer chance rather than his own resourcefulness or courage. It is also a vivid dramatization of the apparent pleasure that some take in killing others. In recent years a debate has opened up between historians such as Christopher Browning, on the one hand, who argues that most of the killers were not German but recruits from lands previously occupied by the Soviets (particularly Ukrainians, Latvians and Lithuanians), and Daniel J. Goldhagen, on the other, who asserts that 'ordinary Germans' were often 'willing executioners'.[24] The film itself anticipates these debates and puts them into a sort of context when captured ss soldiers plead for their lives on the grounds that they are not Germans and were acting under orders: Kosach simply shoots the lot of them. Klimov is not interested in exploring what leads individuals to act with such barbarity: he merely observes its brutalizing effects on one protagonist. The major difference between *Come and See* and *Saving Private Ryan*, however, is that while the latter represents history in terms of individual agency – the rescue of one man, it suggests, can make a difference – *Come and See* instead represents history as process. It shows the hopelessness and futility of a protagonist caught up in events over which he has no control and where his actions make no difference. This, perhaps, is the real tragedy of war.

the emergence of an anti-war cinema

The brutality and the indiscriminate nature of violence as depicted in *Come and See* locate the film within a historical lineage of what is generally termed 'anti-war' cinema. This cinema, which is international in its scope, is defined as much by its attitude towards war as it is by actual content. To represent a 'true' or 'authentic' picture of combat is not necessarily to make an anti-war film: *Saving Private Ryan*, for all its carnage, does not suggest that the Second World War was anything other than necessary and just. An anti-war film is one that expresses, through either its content or its form, the idea of war as a moral tragedy and a waste of human lives. To the extent that it is an attempt to persuade audiences of the tragedy and atrocity of war, then an anti-war film is just as much a piece of propaganda as a gung-ho patriotic combat movie. Indeed, we might say that *All Quiet on the Western Front* was more effective propaganda for peace than, say, *The Green Berets* was propaganda in support of the Vietnam War. The expression of anti-war and pacifist sentiments in film (I am not suggesting, by the way, that all anti-war films are necessarily pacifist) tends to associate this lineage with oppositional or anti-establishment tendencies in film culture. As we shall see, however, the anti-war film has been very much part of the mainstream: major film industries, including Hollywood, have produced cycles of anti-war films that have won popular as well as critical acclaim. These cycles tend to be historically and culturally specific and need to be seen in the context of wider social and political attitudes towards war at different times.

Micheal T. Isenberg, for example, argues that what might be the first genuine cycle of anti-war films was produced in Hollywood in 1915–16 and was very much influenced by American public opinion that wanted to stay out of the war in Europe. Epics such as Thomas Ince's *Civilization* and D. W. Griffith's *Intolerance* and other, lesser-known films such as *In the Name of the Prince of Peace* were nothing if not didactic in asserting their pacifist credentials: these films all draw upon Christian imagery to make somewhat heavy-handed statements about peace. Isenberg suggests that they exhibit a Victorian sense of gentility in their declared abhorrence of war and their endorsement of civilization over barbarism, as well as being influenced by the policy of neutrality adopted by President Woodrow Wilson.[25] This cycle came to an end, however, with the United States' entry into the war, whereupon Hollywood performed a volte-face and turned out a cycle of bellicose anti-German melodramas, such as *Daughter of France* and *The Beast of Berlin*, in 1917–18. The fact that the film industry could switch from anti-war to pro-war films within such a short period of time might seem to suggest that the pacifist sentiments expressed in the earlier films were not entirely sincere. This would probably be unfair. The industry was responding to changing political circumstances and the ideology that consistently underlies commercial film-making is that of the box office.

The response of individual film-makers to the Great War, like that of painters, poets and novelists, produced some distinctive and extremely moving works. This is most apparent in French cinema, where film-makers had greater latitude in using the medium as a mode of personal expression. Abel Gance, for example, who had served as a cinematographer during the war, was inspired to make *J'accuse* (1919) following the deaths of so many of his friends on the Western Front. *J'accuse* is notable less for its rather conventional story – a melodrama focusing on two Frenchmen both in love with the same woman who falls pregnant after being raped whilst in German captivity – than for its powerful and surrealistic imagery. The ending of the film has one of its protagonists, driven mad by shellshock, summoning up the spirits of the dead: their broken and disfigured bodies rise from the grave to confront the civilians who had cheered them on their way to the front ('My name is Jean Diaz, but I have changed my Muse! My dulcet name of yesterday has become "J'accuse"!'). The inspiration for this scene has been found in Gance's wartime diary. In 1916 he wrote: 'How I wish that all those killed in the war would rise up one night and return to their countries, their homes, to see if their sacrifice was worth anything at all. The war would stop of its own accord, horrified by its own awfulness.'[26] *J'accuse*, released shortly after the Armistice, was also shown to great acclaim abroad. Its success can probably be attributed to the public's mood of relief at the end of the war and the sentiment, widespread throughout Europe, that it had been 'a war to end all war'.

Gance's contemporary Jean Renoir, who served as a cavalryman and aviator, similarly based his masterpiece *La Grande Illusion* (1937) on wartime experiences:

> The story of *La Grande Illusion* is absolutely true and was told to me by some of my comrades in the war . . . I

am obviously referring to the war of 1914. In 1914, Hitler had not yet appeared. Nor had the Nazis, who almost succeeded in making people forget that the Germans are also human beings. In 1914, men's spirits had not yet been warped by totalitarian religions and racism. In certain ways, that world war was still a war of formal people, of educated people – I would almost dare say, a gentleman's war. That does not excuse it. Politeness, even chivalry, does not excuse massacre.[27]

La Grande Illusion is perhaps the most sincere and moving statement of Renoir's humanism: its faith in the strength of social bonds and basic human needs across national boundaries is a powerful argument for peaceful coexistence between nations. Renoir, however, later felt that the film had failed in its message: 'In 1936 [*sic*] I made a film called *La Grande Illusion* in which I tried to express all my deep feelings for the cause of peace. This film was very successful. Three years later the war broke out.'[28]

J'accuse and *La Grande Illusion* were, respectively, the first and last films about the Great War made between the Armistice and the outbreak of the Second World War. During this time the production of war-related films fluctuated, though more films, especially during the 1920s, were informed by the experience of war, even if they did not specifically concern the combat experience. Films of the 1920s for the most part acknowledged the losses of the war but accepted that it had been necessary: to this extent *J'accuse* was an isolated example of an anti-war film. War subjects were scarce in French and German film until the late

La Grande Illusion (Jean Renoir, 1937).

1920s. The treatment of war in British films such as *The Guns of Loos* (1928) and *Blighty* (1926) was determined largely by the conventions of melodrama and star performance. Hollywood's first serious engagement with the war, King Vidor's *The Big Parade* (1925), was one of the most successful films of the decade and suggested that audiences were prepared to accept a critical perspective towards war. It was the tenth anniversary of the Armistice, however, that saw the beginning of an international cycle of films – French, German, British and American – that displayed a much more bitter and cynical view of the war. They included *Verdun* (1928), *Westfront 1918* (1930), *Journey's End* (1930), *All Quiet on the Western Front* (1930), *Tell England* (1931), *No Man's Land* (*Niemandsland*, 1931) and *The Wooden Crosses* (*Les Croix de bois*, 1932). The appearance of these films, which share much common ground in subject matter and theme, within such a short period suggests that they can legitimately be seen as a distinct production cycle, even though they spanned different national cinemas.

How can we account for the appearance of this cycle at this time? One reason is that it was not until the middle or late 1920s that the public began to appreciate the horror of war, especially on the Western Front, as more first-hand accounts, no longer subject to censorship, emerged. To this extent, as Pierre Sorlin suggests, 'knowledge of the horrors of the war was a grim secret whose communication was delayed'.[29] This was also the period during which an anti-war literature flourished, exemplified by the publication of fictional and factual accounts including Edmund Blunden's *Undertones of War* (1928), Ernest Hemingway's *A Farewell to Arms* (1929), Richard Aldington's *Death of a Hero* (1929), Robert Graves's *Goodbye To All That* (1929), Siegfried Sassoon's *Memoirs of an Infantry Officer* (1930) and Vera Brittain's *Testament of Youth* (1933). The films *All Quiet on the Western Front*, *Westfront 1918*, *Tell England* and *The Wooden Crosses* were all based on books (by Erich Maria Remarque, Ernst Johannsen, Ernest Raymond and Roland Dorgelès, respectively), and *Journey's End* was adapted from the play by R. C. Sherriff. These books, and the films based on them, can also be seen as part of the culture of remembrance that emerged in the 1920s. The need to come to terms with the losses suffered during the war – ten million dead and many more physically maimed or psychologically scarred – was expressed through literature, painting, music and, above all, the building of war memorials in almost every city, town and village that had lost sons in the war. Jay Winter has brilliantly analysed how these sites of memory and mourning represented a process 'whereby Europeans tried to find ways to comprehend and then to transcend the catastrophes of war'.[30] The appearance of a cycle of anti-war films following the tenth anniversary of the Armistice can be seen as part of this process: film-makers were responding to the public mood and turning to subjects that struck a chord with audiences. To this extent the anti-war cinema was partly informed by commercial considerations. It is significant that it declined later in the 1930s as public opinion changed.

Another factor that influenced the appearance of this cycle at this particular moment was the advent of talking pictures in the late 1920s. *Verdun* was originally a silent film but was reissued with a soundtrack in 1932; the other films in the cycle were all talkies. The addition of sound made the expression of anti-war sentiments more naturalistic since actors could speak about the experiences of their characters. 'More importantly,' adds Samuel Hynes, 'the noise of battle could be reproduced . . . The volume of noise did more than add to the realism: it altered the balance in war films between men and the machinery of war.'[31] It is sometimes held that early talking pictures were primitive in their sound technology, but these films were notable for a level of technological innovation that belies that impression. In *Journey's End*, for example, the constant distant rumble of the artillery was achieved by shaking sheets of metal off camera: the effect is eerie and highly effective. *All Quiet on the Western Front* and *Westfront 1918* were both praised for their aural authenticity, not least in the staccato death rattle of machine guns that reinforces the mechanical nature of modern warfare.

The production and reception histories of all these films, especially *All Quiet on the Western Front*, have been thoroughly

All Quiet on the Western Front (1930).

documented elsewhere.[32] They were, for the most part, critically well received, particularly within the intellectual film culture emerging in Europe at the time. They were, however, subject to the whims of censorial intervention and changing political contexts. Both *All Quiet on the Western Front* and *Westfront 1918*, for example, were banned in Germany following the Nazis' accession to power in 1933. While there are significant stylistic and aesthetic differences between the films – the battlefield panoramas of *All Quiet on the Western Front*, recreated at great expense on the Universal Pictures backlot, are very different from the claustrophobic studio interiors of the far more theatrical *Journey's End* – they do share similar themes and content. Most of the films focus on the experiences of the common soldier in the trenches. (The exceptions are the British films *Journey's End* and *Tell England*, whose protagonists are officers.) All the films eschew heroics and instead focus on the day-to-day life of the men in the trenches. There is little sense of fighting for a cause: when patriotic sentiments are expressed it is usually to expose the hubris behind them. Instead, there is an acute sense of alienation and disillusionment. Soldiers feel they have nothing in common with civilians and that they have no clear reason for fighting other than vague notions of doing their duty. Most remarkable is that, in stark contrast to the propaganda films produced during the war itself, there is no hatred for the enemy. *The Big Parade* and *All Quiet on the Western Front*, for example, both include scenes where their main protagonist finds himself sharing a foxhole with an enemy soldier. *Westfront 1918* ends with a French soldier in a military hospital reaching out for the hand of the dying German next to him and saying 'Moi comrade, pas enemie' ('My comrade, not enemy'). (In his next film, *Kameradschaft*, the director, G. W. Pabst, similarly explored the theme of Franco-German reconciliation through the story of a mine rescue: *Kameradschaft* is not strictly a war film but has affinities with *Westfront 1918*.) The overriding impression created by all the films is of the futility and waste of war. *All Quiet on the Western Front*, *Westfront 1918*, *Journey's End*, *Tell England* and *The Wooden Crosses* all end in the deaths of one or more of their protagonists. And *Verdun*, *All Quiet on the Western Front* and *The Wooden Crosses* all close with a haunting image of the landscape covered in white crosses – a shot that would become a recurring motif of First World War films.

What is the historical significance of these films? On one level they were responsible, in large measure, for establishing a visual iconography of the First World War that persists to the present day. The recurring images are devastated landscapes with ruins of buildings and broken tree trunks, tangled fences of barbed wire and, above all, mud: one could be forgiven for thinking that the

First World War was fought entirely in the rain. No matter that films like *The Battle of the Somme* show the landscape as scorched and dusty: a film somehow does not seem authentic unless the combatants are caked in mud or wading knee-deep in dirty water. In fact, this is a partial and selective view of the war. It might be an accurate image of some sectors of the Western Front, but other theatres were not characterized by the stalemate of trench warfare. What the films represent, perhaps, is a visual imagining of the war rather than an accurate picture of it. They picture what Siegfried Sassoon described as the 'veritable gloom and disaster of the thing called Armageddon . . . a dreadful place, a place of horror and desolation which no imagination could have invented'.[33]

As well as inventing the visual iconography of the war, the films also influenced the psychological response to it. Their recurring theme is that 'war is hell'. It is an entirely catastrophic experience that leaves its protagonists traumatized both mentally and physically. Although the idea of 'shell shock' as a medical condition was contested at the time, the films demonstrate its effects through their representation of the stress experienced by men under bombardment. The central protagonists of *Westfront 1918* and *Journey's End* have become alcoholics: drink is a metaphor of their descent into madness. A recurring motif of the films is that of the young recruit who realizes that his dreams of martial glory are illusory when he arrives at the front. *All Quiet on the Western Front*, *Journey's End* and *Tell England* dramatize how idealistic youths are transformed into bitter veterans: 'This is what I'd like to tell England!' cries the protagonist of the last film as he dies in agony. The disillusionment of war is most

All Quiet on the Western Front.

vividly expressed in the scene from *All Quiet on the Western Front* where Paul Bäumer (Lew Ayres) returns to his old school on leave and is asked by the schoolmaster who had persuaded him to enlist to tell of his heroic deeds. He replies: 'We live with the rats – we burrow like rabbits – and we try not to be killed – but most of us are . . . There's no glory in the mud.' Paul comes to welcome the prospect of death as a release from the trauma: 'There's only one thing worse than dying out there – and that's living out there.'

The films also had a significant role to play in the cultural politics of commemoration and remembrance. The theme of the 'lost generation' is prominent. The opening of *All Quiet on the Western Front* reproduces the book's dedication to 'a generation of men, who, even though they may have escaped its shells, were destroyed by the war'. Sorlin points out that, since so many First World War films end in death, with few if any survivors, 'nobody cares to tell what happened and there is no memory . . . The emptiness of the shots give [*sic*] them an impact, an intensity that tends to overwhelm the spectator and make us feel we have been caught up in some vast, impersonal, meaningless disaster.'[34] In this sense the imagery of the films is being used to reinforce their ideological position: the futility and waste of war. It is impossible to read the films in any other way. They are so highly didactic that they do not allow space for contested readings. This is one reason why *La Grande Illusion* – which does not refer to this visual iconography of war – stands somewhat apart from the rest of the cycle.

Perhaps the most significant feature of the cycle, however, is its internationalism. Each of the major combatant nations contributed to the cycle. (Or, rather, each of the major combatant nations that was a democracy after the war contributed: the Fascist regime in Italy from 1922 made anything other than the glorification of the nation's war record impossible, while the Soviet Union was preoccupied during the 1920s with its own ideological project of promoting an approved image of the Bolshevik revolution rather than with the 'imperialist' war.) The films themselves suggest a universal experience of the war that transcends national boundaries. *All Quiet on the Western Front*, an American film of a German novel, was the most successful of the cycle. The British Board of Film Censors considered it a 'wonderfully realistic representation [of] war with minimum

national bias'.[35] Another example of the ease with which representations of war crossed national boundaries is that a German
adaptation of *Journey's End*, though maintaining its British characters, was produced only a year later as *The Other Side* (*Die
Andere Seite*, 1931). While both films are faithful adaptations that
stick closely to the dialogue of the play, there are subtle but significant differences between them. Mostly these concern the
characterization of the principal protagonist, Stanhope, arising
from the different cultural contexts of the British theatre and
German cinema. The performance of Colin Clive in *Journey's
End* is highly theatrical: his Stanhope is stoical, fatalistic, cynical,
repressed, neurotic. In *The Other Side*, however, Conrad Veidt
brings an altogether more physical style of performance to the
part, characterized by his asymmetrical body movements and an
intense gaze fixed on a point behind the camera. Whereas Clive
turns his back to the camera at moments of heightened expression, as if attempting to hide his anguish, Veidt fixes his gaze on
the spectator who is thereby drawn into the psychological world
of the drama rather than remaining a detached observer. The
concluding shot of each film sums up these differences. In both
films the dugout is hit by a shell and everyone within is killed,
though in *Journey's End* the shot is from inside and Clive turns
away from the camera at the moment of the explosion – the film
shies away from showing the expression of death – whereas in *The
Other Side* the shot is from outside the dugout and Veidt is
advancing towards the camera, *Caligari*-like, when the shell hits.
In her study of German war films of the Weimar period,

Bernadette Kester suggests that Stanhope's life is 'spared': while we do not see him die, however, it seems to me that his death is implied.[36]

The decision to maintain the play's British perspective in *The Other Side*, even to the extent of referring to the Germans as 'Huns', is significant. Kester speculates whether 'such a film, from a German military perspective, could ever have been made in Germany'.[37] The *Dolchstosslegende* – the view that the German army had not been defeated in the field in 1918 but rather had been betrayed by politicians in Berlin – was not merely an invention of National Socialist propaganda: to this extent it was, perhaps, expedient to suggest that British officers were breaking down under the stress of war rather than their German counterparts. In any event the election of Hitler in 1933 and the control of the German film industry exercised by the Reich Propaganda Minister Dr Joseph Goebbels signalled an end to the production of any films that might be considered anti-war or defeatist. *All Quiet on the Western Front* and *The Other Side* were on the list of films banned in Germany after 1933. The Nazi accession to power was one of several factors that signalled a shift in the popular representation of war. The emergence of an international anti-war cinema had been made possible by a combination of cultural, social and political circumstances in the late 1920s and early 1930s, but as those circumstances changed in the mid-1930s the cycle petered out. The ascendancy of Fascism in Germany and Italy was one factor: these regimes did not tolerate expression of pacifist or anti-war sentiments. In Britain and France, moreover, censorship became more stringent during the 1930s and film producers were discouraged from tackling controversial subject matter. And when Universal Pictures produced the sequel to *All Quiet on the Western Front*, *The Road Back* (1937), much of the anti-war dialogue was removed at the insistence of the Production Code Administration in response to complaints from the German consul.[38]

The First World War disappeared from cinemas for much of the 1940s and '50s: the Second World War was a more immediate historical experience. In the late 1950s and '60s, however, a second major cycle of films about the Western Front appeared, including *Paths of Glory* (1957), *The Great War* (*La Grande guerra*, 1959), *King and Country* (1964) and *Oh! What a Lovely War* (1969). As with the earlier cycle there were specific historical and cultural reasons for the appearance of these films at this time. This was the period that saw the emergence of various 'new wave' movements in the film industries of Europe that promoted a more personalized mode of film-making around the personality of the director or *auteur*. A characteristic of many new-wave cinemas was that they adopted a more irreverent and cynical attitude towards cherished national myths and popular narratives of the past. There was also, at this time, a renewed popular and historical interest in the First World War, occasioned by the fiftieth anniversary of its outbreak in 1964. The major BBC2 series *The Great War* (1964) and the publication of popular histories such as Alan Clark's *The Donkeys* and Leon Wolff's *In Flanders Fields* encouraged a view of the war that still persists. The terrible losses of the Western Front were attributed to poor tactics and incompetent leadership. The generals were held responsible for sending millions of brave men to their deaths ('lions led by donkeys') and for prolonging the war through their adherence to outmoded tactics. A combination of these factors – a new generation of younger film-makers unafraid to court controversy and a popular view of the war in which the officer class was held responsible for the carnage of the trenches – influenced the style of these films.

In their visual representation of the war, the films of the 1950s and '60s look back to the iconography established by the earlier films: trenches and mud. *King and Country* was even released in sepia-tinted prints to resemble more closely the style of contemporary visual records of the war. *Oh! What a Lovely War* concludes with a familiar image of a landscape of white crosses stretching as far as the eye can see. The films therefore locate themselves in relation to an existing visual image of the war that would be recognizable to their audiences. What is different about these films, however, is their acute awareness of class difference. To a large degree this was a consequence of the 'cultural revolution' of the 1960s: social change in Western Europe and North America brought about the end of deference and gave a voice to the working classes that had long been denied them in popular culture. In *Paths of Glory*, *King and Country* and *Oh! What a Lovely War* there is none of the sympathy for the *ancien régime* that had characterized *La Grande Illusion*. These films set up systematic and highly didactic oppositions between officers (upper class, effete, public-school-educated, privileged) and enlisted men (working class, proletarian, often uneducated, always underprivileged) that conforms to the 'lions led by donkeys' myth.

Paths of Glory
(Stanley Kubrick,
1957).

King and Country
(Joseph Losey, 1964).

They all suggest a vast social divide between the general staff, who are seen living a life of luxury and opulence in magnificent chââteaux far behind the lines, and the men in the trenches, who suffer squalor, disease and starvation and the ever-present threat of death from either the enemy or their own artillery.

Paths of Glory and *King and Country* both expose the hypocrisy of military justice. In the former three French soldiers are shot as scapegoats for the failure of an assault, and in the latter a soldier court martialled for desertion has to be shot by the officer who had defended him in court. In both films, it is suggested, the real war is a class war. There is a radical edge to the social politics of these films that had been entirely absent from the earlier cycle. Their representation of military (in)justice has shaped popular views of the war to the extent that *King and Country* has been cited in the campaign to pardon those who were 'shot at dawn'.[39] And the radical social politics of the films have proved influential on later film treatments of the war, such as *Regeneration* (1996) and *The Trench* (1997).

The most ambitious, yet least regarded, of the 'second wave' of Great War films was Richard Attenborough's production of Joan Littlewood's play *Oh! What a Lovely War*. The reception of the film was exemplified by David Wilson's review in the *Monthly Film Bulletin*, which called it 'a worthy mosaic of bits and pieces, full of good ideas but nowhere near to being a self-contained dramatic entity'.[40] Where it differs from the previous films is in its adoption of a non-naturalistic style of presentation: hitherto, the experience of the trenches had been dramatized in realistic mode. *Oh! What a Lovely War* imagines the war as a variety show staged on Brighton Pier, advertised with the slogan: 'World War One – battles, songs and a few jokes'. The presentation of war as a form of entertainment is perhaps a comment on the nature of the war film as much as it is an attack on the conduct of the war itself. It is significant as the only feature film (at least to my knowledge) that examines the causes of the war – interpreted here as a squabble amongst the crowned heads of Europe

Oh! What a Lovely War (Richard Attenborough, 1969).

– though its main intent is to expose the incompetence and blinkered stupidity of the generals. The film subverts expectations by casting John Mills, the decent upstanding hero of a dozen British war movies, as a blustering and buffoonish Field Marshal Sir Douglas Haig. It is a popular impression of Haig that still persists, despite the efforts of revisionist historians.[41]

The historian Gary Sheffield has suggested that most people's impressions of the First World War 'view it as a unique cultural event, essentially "outside" history'.[42] This, to some degree at least, is a consequence of film and other popular representations. Although films such as *All Quiet on the Western Front* and *Westfront 1918* have a clear temporal location, it seems to matter less than their universal and, in a sense, timeless images of the trenches. To a modern viewer the historical context of *Journey's End*, set immediately before the German Army's Spring Offensive of March 1918, seems largely irrelevant: the events could have taken place at almost any point between 1915 and 1918. *Oh! What a Lovely War* condenses four years of war into just over two hours and ends with an impression of continued deadlock rather than the successful Allied offensive that brought the war to a conclusion.

As Niall Ferguson observes: 'It is not from historians that the majority of modern readers gain their impressions of the First World War, but from books . . . and, of course, from newspapers, television, theatre and cinema'.[43] Ninety years after the events themselves, when only a handful of the survivors remain, the 'memory' of the war persists through its representation in popular culture. The abiding visual image of the war remains that of *All Quiet on the Western Front* and the popular historical impression that of *Oh! What a Lovely War*: a million men sacrificed through the incompetence and stupidity of the generals. This cinematic historiography has become so dominant that it informs national cinemas beyond Europe, exemplified by Peter Weir's *Gallipoli* (1981), which places the blame for the decimation of the ANZACs (Australian and New Zealand Army Corps) squarely at the door of upper-class British officers. And it persists in television representations of the war, ranging from serious dramas such as Alan Bleasdale's *The Monocled Mutineer* (1987) – a drama-documentary account of a British army mutiny at Etaples in 1917 – to the popular comedy series *Blackadder Goes Forth* (1989), which combined the British tradition of vulgar comedy with a bitter satire of military incompetence: a sort of *Carry On Up the Somme*.[44] *The Monocled Mutineer* caused a storm of controversy and was savagely attacked by sections of the right-wing press: to date it has not been repeated.[45] More recently, *The Somme: From Defeat to Victory* (2006) offered a revisionist interpretation of British army tactics between the early and later phases of the protracted battle. It is doubtful, however, that the efforts of the revisionists will succeed in reclaiming the popular image of the First World War from the myth of 'lions led by donkeys' forged in the films of the 1960s.

war and memory

In recent years the notion of 'popular memory' or 'cultural memory' has become voguish in the study of the past. This refers not so much to the actual memories of individuals (though the recording of the personal experiences of 'ordinary' people is the aim of major oral history projects such as the BBC's 'People's War'), but rather to the idea of a shared set of views and beliefs about the past. It refers to 'the things that people implicitly believe rather than what historians tell them'.[46] Such 'memory' tends to be nationally specific and generally revolves around significant episodes in the national past. In Britain, for example, the popular memory of the Second World War is that of 'standing alone' against Hitler and privileges the events of 1940: Dunkirk, the Battle of Britain and the Blitz. And, as we have seen, *Saving Private Ryan* represents the American popular memory of the sacrifice of a generation of young US servicemen 'on the altar of freedom'. Anglo-American narratives of the Second World War tend to represent it as 'the good war': one that was fought in a righteous cause to protect democracy and to destroy the evil of National Socialism. However, in countries like France, which experienced German occupation, or in those East European states that witnessed the full horrors of Nazi genocide, the Second World War gives rise to a very different memory. It is generally one that is unfamiliar to Western publics: *Come and See*, for example, dramatizes what the film's publicity materials referred to as the 'little-known holocaust' of Belorussia. The fact that so much of Eastern Europe came under Soviet domination after the war further complicates the role of memory in those countries. East European commentators such as the Croatian Dubravka Ugrešić have written of 'the confiscation of memory' following the collapse of Communism and the end of the Cold War.[47]

The filmic historiography of the Second World War as represented in the cinemas of continental Europe demonstrates the extent to which popular memory is bitterly contested. Nowhere is this better demonstrated than by the example of Poland. Of all the cinemas in the post-war Soviet sphere of influence, Poland was the most resistant to the control of Moscow and to the aesthetic doctrine of Socialist Realism. The popular memory of the Second World War, as represented in Polish cinema, cast the Poles as victims of German/Fascist aggression. That they were also the victims of Soviet duplicity could only be hinted at. The Warsaw Uprising of 1944 was celebrated in Polish narratives of resistance, but the fact that the uprising was led by the (non-communist) Home Army and that the Red Army halted outside Warsaw while the Germans suppressed it were taboo subjects. Thus the first Polish film about the uprising, Aleksander Ford's *Border Street* (*Ulica graniczna*, 1948), does not identify the partisans as either nationalists or communists. It also ignores the existence of anti-Semitism by presenting a narrative of unity between Poles and Jews in their resistance to the occupying Germans. The equivocation in the film was enough to condemn it in the eyes of one Communist Party critic, who complained that 'the identity of the people aiding the Ghetto is presented as quite anonymous in this film'.[48]

Border Street is technically crude in parts, caused largely by the impoverished conditions under which it was produced, but it was prestigious enough for Film Polski, the nationalized state film industry, to enter it in the Venice Film Festival, where Ford won a gold award. For distribution in English-speaking countries an introduction was added by the American journalist and broadcaster Quentin Reynolds. Reynolds's voice had been a familiar feature of wartime British propaganda documentaries such as *London Can Take It!* and *Christmas Under Fire*, in which he valorized the stoicism of the British public during the Blitz – largely for American consumption. His introductory voice-over ('It is easy for tyrants to kill the bodies of men, it is more difficult for them to kill the dreams of men') expressed a very similar sentiment to his commentary for *London Can Take It!* ('A bomb has its limitations. It can only destroy buildings and kill people. It cannot kill the unconquerable spirit and courage of the people of London.') Yet despite this, British critics found the film 'too crude to leave the audience with more than a sense of guilt at being comparatively unmoved by so much suffering'.[49]

For all its limitations, however, *Border Street* anticipated the more successful films of Andrzej Wajda. We have already seen how Wajda's 'war trilogy' exhibits a tendency towards symbolism and away from realism; this aesthetic shift mirrors another in the politics of the films. The conventional interpretation of the trilogy is to see it as reflecting a trajectory from an ideologically correct narrative of anti-Fascist resistance (*A Generation*, 1954) to a celebration of the role of the Home Army during the Warsaw Uprising (*Kanal*, 1956) to an ambiguous affirmation of anti-communism at the end of the war (*Ashes and Diamonds*, 1958).[50] Wajda had fought in the Home Army and it is difficult not to read the films from an autobiographical perspective. While there are subtle ideological differences between them, all three films are characterized by a mood of fatalism: their protagonists are caught up in events beyond their control. That Wajda could make films that did not glorify heroism, in contrast to the cinema of Socialist Realism prevailing elsewhere in the Eastern bloc, was due largely to the more independent (from Moscow control) government of Wladyslaw Gomulka, who became First Secretary of the Polish Workers' Party in 1956.

Wajda's films are characterized by their powerful imagery, psychological intensity and allegorical content. *A Generation* is set in 1942 and focuses on two teenagers, Janek and Stach, who join a resistance group led by Dorita, a young woman to whom Stach is attracted. The film ends with Janek dead, Dorita caught by the Gestapo and Stach assuming leadership of the resistance cell. *A Generation* won admirers abroad for its 'purity of style', but pleased neither the authorities nor the public at home: critics found it 'too half-hearted' as anti-Fascist propaganda, whereas Polish audiences seem to have been upset that it made no reference to Soviet duplicity.[51] *Kanal*, set, like the conclusion of

Border Street, during the Warsaw Uprising, is a grim tale of fatalistic heroism that portrays the members of the Home Army in stubborn, heroic mould. The increased stylization that Western critics disliked can be seen as part of Wajda's strategy to express visually what he could not state directly. Towards the end of the film, for example, the partisan Stokrotka stares out through an iron grille at the banks of the Vistula: the empty space where, in reality, the Red Army had halted while it waited for the Germans to crush the uprising. The meaning is clear: the film is blaming the failure of the uprising on the inaction of the Soviets. The critic John Simon thought *Kanal* 'as perfect an anti-war film as was ever made'.[52]

The sense of disillusion suggested in *A Generation* and emerging in *Kanal* pervades *Ashes and Diamonds*. The critic Peter John Dyer commented upon Wajda's 'gift for disillusioned passion and tragedy'.[53] *Ashes and Diamonds* is set during May 1945, in the days immediately after the German surrender, and focuses on Maciek, a Home Army resistance fighter ordered by

Kanal (Andrzej Wajda, 1956).

his superiors to assassinate a Soviet-trained official of the Polish puppet government. The first attempt is a failure and two innocent people are killed; a second attempt succeeds, but Maciek is shot dead by Russian troops. *Ashes and Diamonds* is decidedly anti-heroic in tone, suggesting that the idealism of the wartime resistance has been betrayed by the political exigencies of the post-war settlement. That the film is an allegory of the present as well as a narrative of the past is evident in Maciek's remark: 'The fight for Poland, the fight for what sort of country it's going to be, has only just started. And each one of us may be killed – any day.'

The divisive legacy of the war continued to inform Polish cinema throughout later decades. Andrzej Munk died before completing *Passenger* (1963), which looked back at the Holocaust through the eyes of Liza, a German who had been an ss guard at Auschwitz. The film was completed by others according to Munk's intentions: its fragmented narrative has been interpreted as a reflection of the difficulty of remembering the Holocaust.[54] *Passenger* is a powerful, haunting film that deserves comparison to more celebrated works such as Alain Resnais's *Hiroshima, mon amour* (a meditation on the nature of memory) and Liliana Cavani's *The Night Porter* (an exploration of the co-dependent relationships that develop between concentration camp inmates and guards). In *Landscape After Battle* (1970), Wajda explored post-war dislocation through the story of a concentration camp survivor who finds himself confined to an American-run displaced persons camp. Its protagonist, who belongs nowhere, has been interpreted as an allegory for the Polish experience of liberation from National Socialism, only to face further subjugation under Communism.[55]

Passenger (Andrzej Munk and Witold Lesiewicz, 1963).

The level of political dissent evident in Polish cinema was less apparent elsewhere in the Eastern bloc. In the German Democratic Republic (GDR), for example, the state film organization DEFA (Deutsche Film Aktiengesellschaft) maintained a rigorous control over content and style. DEFA was less favourably inclined towards *auteur* cinema and encouraged a practice of collective film-making. The ideological project of East German cinema, especially during the 1950s and '60s, was the critical examination of the Fascist past and its implications for the present. Konrad Wolf's *Sterne* (1958), for example, was one of the first films to attempt to 'explain' the Holocaust, though it resorts to melodramatic conventions to do so. Joachim Kunert's *The Adventures of Werner Holt* (*Die Abenteuer des Werner Holt*, 1965) is a narrative of ideological conversion that presses home its anti-war theme as its protagonist, indoctrinated with National Socialism by his schoolmaster, comes to realize the senselessness of war. Shot in the crisp monochrome that characterizes the visual style of DEFA, the film represents the battlefield as a landscape scarred by the machinery of war: images of wrecked and burning vehicles abound.

Sabine Hake argues that the modernist style that emerged in East German cinema in the 1960s 'provided film-makers with an analytical framework for challenging established views on the origins of fascism, the legacies of anti-fascism and the impact of recent political events on the self-undertaking of the GDR as both the "real" and the "other" Germany'.[56] These themes are most fully explored in Konrad Wolf's *I Was Nineteen* (*Ich war neunzehn*, 1968), an autobiographical film focusing on Gregor, a young German-born lieutenant raised in Russia who returns to Germany with the Red Army during the last weeks of the war. Wolf, son of the playwright Friedrich Wolf, had emigrated with his parents when the Nazis came to power and lived in exile in Moscow: like his protagonist he served in the Red Army towards the end of the war. Unlike his contemporary Wajda, however, Wolf cannot be constructed as an oppositional figure: as a Communist Party member and President of the Academy of Artists, indeed, he was closely associated with the regime. *I Was Nineteen* is an extended commentary on the legacy of National Socialism in which various discursive strategies are employed. At different points in the film a diverse range of characters attempt to account for Hitler's rise to power. These range from an intellectual who sees it in terms of a psychological disposition towards authoritarianism ('a trait of our people before Hitler . . . an artificially induced frenzy of obedience') to a socialist schoolteacher who explains it through conventional Marxism ('He was empowered by industrialists, big corporations, the German army . . . They gave Hitler and the Nazis the power he wanted'). Like other DEFA films, it is characterized by striking visuals that reinforce the

The Jackboot Mutiny (G. W. Pabst, 1955).

cruelty of war: it opens with a panorama of an icy river down which floats a raft on which a German soldier hangs from a gallows with a placard declaring 'Deserter! I licked Russian boots'. This 'citation' from Rossellini's *Paisa* is one of several references in the film, which also include *La Grande Illusion* in a sequence where Gregor tries to negotiate the surrender of a German stronghold in Spandau castle.[57]

The historical memory of the German Federal Republic (GFR) during the 1950s was problematic in a different way. The GFR's inclusion within the Council of Europe (1951), NATO (1955) and the European Economic Community (1958) marked its political rehabilitation in the eyes of the Western Allies. GFR cinema has sometimes been accused of ignoring social and political realities – a charge levelled by the signatories of the Oberhausen Manifesto in 1962 – and of failing to engage with the legacy of National Socialism. This charge is unfair. West German cinema had an ideological project of its own that was to negotiate the tension between the Nazi past and the anti-communist ideology of the Cold War. In the early 1950s, it would be true to say, audiences had to be satisfied with Hollywood representations of Germany's war such as *The Desert Fox* (1951), in which James Mason gave a sympathetic portrait of Field Marshal Erwin Rommel as a decent and honourable soldier whose growing disillusion with the Nazis brings him into opposition with Hitler and ultimately results in his arrest and suicide. This is also the model for early West German war films such as *The Devil's General* (*Des Teufels General*, 1955) and *The Jackboot Mutiny* (*Es geschah am 20. Juli*, 1955), which focused on internal resistance to the Nazi regime within the military. *The Devil's General*, directed by Helmut Käutner from a play by Carl Zuckmayer, is a fictional story about a German air-force general who becomes disillusioned with Nazism. The film reinterpreted its source material to offer a more pro-American, anti-communist orientation.[58] *The Jackboot Mutiny*, the penultimate film by G. W. Pabst, is an account of the bomb plot of July 1944 when Colonel von Stauffenberg narrowly failed to assassinate Hitler in the Wolf's Lair. The film characterizes the conspirators, led by General von Beck, as German patriots who regard it as their duty to save the nation from Hitlerism. It is a disappointingly dull film – Pabst's visual flair is constrained by the semi-documentary mode adopted for factually based historical re-enactment – and it was not a box-office success.[59]

In the later 1950s West German film-makers adopted different narrative strategies for representing the war. *The Star of Africa* (*Der Stern von Afrika*, 1957) and *U47 – Lieutenant Commander Prien* (*U47 – Kapitänleutnant Prien*, 1958) dramatized stories of individual heroism that maintained a suitable ideologi-

Punishment Battalion 999 (Harald Philipp, 1959).

cal and geographical distance from the regime. The dramatic conventions of these films are not far removed from the propaganda cinema of the Third Reich: the valorization of heroism and the promotion of an ideal of warrior masculinity. The other strategy was the resort to a conventional 'war is hell' theme, such as *The Doctor of Stalingrad* (*Der Arzt von Stalingrad*, 1958) and *Punishment Battalion 999* (*Strafbataillon 999*, 1959). *The Doctor of Stalingrad* focuses on the brutal treatment of German prisoners by their Russian captors: to this extent it was very much a product of the Cold War. The humane doctor was a recurring archetype of West German war films who also appeared in *Punishment Battalion 999*, in which various 'dissidents' (including an officer who allowed his men to retreat rather than be slaughtered and a doctor accused of self-harm in order to avoid conscription when in fact he was trying to find a cure for gangrene) are sent to a penal unit on the Russian Front, where they endure a harsh regime before being sent on a suicidal mission to clear a minefield. Again there is an anti-Soviet theme – Tanya, a young Polish girl working as a nurse, is raped by a

Russian soldier – which locates the film within the ideological coordinates of Cold War propaganda.

The most ambitious, and successful, of West German war films at this time was Frank Wisbar's *Stalingrad* (1958), sometimes also known as *Dogs, Do You Want to Live Forever?* (*Hunde, wollt ihr ewig leben?*). It is a semi-documentary account of the battle that marked the turning point of the war on the Eastern Front in which actuality footage is so seemlessly edited into the dramatic reconstruction that at times it is difficult to identify which is which. *Stalingrad* differentiates between 'good' Germans such as Oberleutnant Gerd Wisse – whose humanity is established in a scene at the beginning of the film, where he finds a job for Katja, a Russian girl in the occupied zone, who otherwise faces deportation to a labour camp – and fanatical Nazis such as Major Linkmann, a strict disciplinarian who declares that 'the Führer needs men of iron to overcome problems'. The film lays the blame for the German defeat at Stalingrad squarely at the door of Hitler's misguided strategy and criticizes the reluctance of General von Paulus, commander-in-chief of the German Sixth Army, to question his orders to stay and fight until it is too late ('Our sacrifice for Stalingrad is a military necessity'). The film asserts its anti-war credentials through dialogue ('This is not a just war. The men die for nothing') and through its striking visuals that create an authentic impression of the bitter cold and harsh conditions endured by the defenders. It also uses irony to great effect, such as the sequence towards the end where a cellar of wounded and dying German troops have to listen to a propaganda broadcast by Goering celebrating the tenth anniversary of the

Third Reich. The film ends with captured German soldiers marching into captivity, some of them dropping dead in the snow. It seems perfectly reasonable to assume that this image would have exerted a powerful effect on German audiences, who would have known only too well that fewer than one in ten of those who surrendered at Stalingrad survived captivity.

Sorlin suggests that the concentration of war films in the GFR in the late 1950s arose from the fact that 'Germany was being progressively reintegrated into the concert of western nations ... The films made in 1954–57 were not blatant propaganda but were merely adapted to the circumstances. Once Germany was rehabilitated the producers abandoned the field.'[60] The war film was much less prominent in West German cinema after the late 1950s, when the production of genre films was dominated by westerns and thrillers. Later war films such as Wolfgang Petersen's *The Boat* (*Das Boot*, 1981) and Joseph Vilsmaier's *Stalingrad* (1991) provide a more detached perspective on the war, free from the ideological climate of the Cold War and made at sufficient remove from events for the issue of war guilt to have faded. They adhere to the same semi-documentary realist conventions as the films of the 1950s and assert their credentials as 'fact', even though both films are distillations of wartime experiences. *The Boat* was acclaimed for its psychological realism – few films achieve such an impression of the strains and stresses of combat – and for the claustrophobic effect achieved by its use of confined spaces and a hand-held camera. But to what extent is it really an anti-war film? Its narrative structure is not dissimilar to the anti-war classic *All Quiet on the Western Front*: the war is seen through the eyes of a

Das Boot (Wolfgang Petersen, 1981).

newcomer (a war correspondent who joins the crew of U-96) who is shocked by his first experience of combat; the action sequences are punctuated by a respite (Christmas dinner); and the film ends with the death of a central protagonist (the captain). Outside Germany, however, there were some who felt that the anti-war credentials of *The Boat* were compromised by commercial imperatives. The *Monthly Film Bulletin*, for example, averred that

> Petersen and his collaborators are so busy looking over their shoulders – 'dealing' with the problem of German guilt by luxuriating in a sense of doom about the enterprise of U-96 and its crew – while looking towards those ex-Allied markets, that they can't begin to investigate the subject in a more honest way.[61]

This seems to me to miss the point: the fact that the protagonists of *The Boat* are German is almost irrelevant, since the genre conventions of the submarine film are common to other national cinemas.

The same cannot be said of *Stalingrad*, a partial remake of the 1958 film that adopts an explicitly anti-war perspective towards this defining moment of the German experience of the Second World War. The episodic narrative follows the members of a platoon transferred from North Africa who find the conduct of war in this theatre more brutalizing than anything they have experienced before. It charts the growing disillusion of a decent, humane young officer whose notions of gentlemanly conduct are brutally dashed. *Stalingrad* is characterized by its vivid realization of the carnage and squalor of combat: a makeshift hospital is as filthy as its inhabitants are bloodied and in one shocking moment the lieutenant falls into a sewer polluted by corpses where rats feed on the dead. The *New York Times* felt that *Stalingrad* 'goes about as far as a movie can go in depicting modern warfare as a stomach-turning form of mass slaughter' – again

Stalingrad (Joseph Vilsmaier, 1993).

demonstrating that *Saving Private Ryan* was far from the first film to do this – and that it 'powerfully underscores the adage that war is hell'.[62] Perhaps the most significant feature of *Stalingrad*, however, is that unlike the film of 1958 it does not avoid the unpalatable fact of atrocities committed by German soldiers, though their actions are blamed on the brutalizing effects of war rather than on the racial ideology of National Socialism. In one scene the three main protagonists discuss without emotion their intent to rape a captive Russian female soldier – they will 'take turns' by rank – though in the event she is spared this fate by the intervention of the young lieutenant, Hans. (It turns out that she has already been molested and feels shame at being 'the German whore – a collaborator'.) The film ends with the girl and two Germans attempting to escape the carnage: trudging through a vast snowscape, they are shot by an unseen sniper. The last shot – of Hans dying in the snow – recalls the conclusion of Robert Altman's revisionist western *McCabe and Mrs Miller*. Yet this fate may have been preferable to captivity. A caption solemnly informs us that of the 91,000 German troops who surrendered at Stalingrad, only 6,000 ever made it home alive.

The defeat at Stalingrad occupies centre-place in the German historical memory of the Second World War: it provides a narrative in which the Germans, too, are victims. The Finnish film *The Winter War* (*Talvisota*, 1990) bears striking similarities to *Stalingrad* both in its images of brutal combat amidst the snow and in its narrative of stubborn resistance. *The Winter War*, however, is an anti-war film only in the sense that it depicts the unpleasantness of the combat experience. Its ideological project is very different: to commemorate the heroism of the small, poorly equipped Finnish army against the Red Army during the Russo-Finnish War of 1939–40. The promotional statement of the film ('They held back the Russian Juggernaut in a frozen Hell!') sums up its content: a grim celebration of national resistance. To this extent *The Winter War* can be understood as part of a process 'to re-evaluate the significance of the Finnish resistance and the sacrifices that were made in 1939 to 1944'.[63]

The role of cinema in constructing and challenging narratives of national history is no better demonstrated than in the case of France. Post-war French cinema promoted a Gaullist myth of the resistance as a national movement – a myth that takes shape as early as Clement's *The Battle of the Rails* (1946) and is still evident some twenty years later in *Is Paris Burning?* (1965). It was not until the 1970s that French film-makers were able to question some aspects of this myth – and even then their efforts to do so aroused much controversy. Marcel Ophüls's *The Sorrow and the Pity* (*Le chagrin et la pitié*, 1970) used a combination of newsreels and interviews to suggest that French people by and large cooperated with the German authorities during the Occupation and turned a blind eye to the deportation of Jews. While the impact of Ophüls's film was limited beyond intellectual circles – its format, a four-hour documentary, meant that it was hardly a commercial prospect – the same cannot be said of Louis Malle's fictional film *Lacombe, Lucien* (1974), which provoked such a storm that Malle was forced to leave France and work in America for the next decade. *Lacombe, Lucien* is the story of a disaffected youth who becomes a collaborator. Malle later said about the controversy around the film:

What makes *Lacombe, Lucien* strong and what made the
controversy somewhat of a series of misunderstandings is
that in its description of characters and events the film
exposes all the ambiguities and contradictions in behaviour that belonged to that period . . . The controversy was
between French intellectuals and politicians. Those who
attacked it did so on the grounds that it was fiction: we had
invented and put on the screen a character who was
complex and ambiguous to the point where his behaviour
was acceptable.[64]

Those intellectuals included Michel Foucault, who perceived
the film as a way of representing a national experience as a
personalized narrative, 'embodying it in a character or a group
of characters who at any given moment represent the essence of
an exceptional relationship with power'.[65] This may be so, but it
does not adequately explain the reaction to the film, which would
seem also to have arisen partly from the suggestion of Fascism as
an attractive and even seductive idea. It is significant in this
regard that Lucien does not become a collaborator through ideological commitment but, rather, is lured by the promise of
money, a gun and sex. The press release for the film described
Lucien as 'un jeune d'aujourd'hui' ('a youth of today'), and to
this extent the controversy might have been prompted by the
apparent inference that contemporary French youth might be
attracted by Fascism.

The critical response to *Lacombe, Lucien* locates the film
within what Foucault called 'the struggle over popular memory'.

It was also part of a trend in the 1970s for films about the Third Reich that demonstrated a more ambivalent attitude towards the nature of National Socialism. Films such as Luchino Visconti's *The Damned* (1970), Liliana Cavani's *The Night Porter* (1974), Lina Wertmüller's *Seven Beauties* (1975), Joseph Losey's *Mr Kline* (1977), Volker Schlöndorff's *The Tin Drum* (1979) and Rainer Werner Fassbinder's *Lili Marleen* (1980) examined power relationships within Nazi Germany or Fascist Italy. The relationships were often expressed in sexual form, as in *The Night Porter* and *Seven Beauties*, focusing on relationships between concentration camp inmates and their captors: the theme here is the co-dependency of each party on the other. This cycle of films can be seen as an exploration of what Susan Sontag, in a famous essay, described as 'fascinating fascism': the extent to which Nazi imagery (particularly uniforms and flags) holds an ambiguous place in popular culture.[66] The films are also invested with 'art cinema' trappings by their *auteur* directors, such as their use of visual stylization and flashback narratives that probe the 'memory' of the Third Reich. Yet, especially in the case of *The Night Porter* and *Seven Beauties*, the films tread perilously close to the tradition of exploitation film-making and sex melodramas that emerged, especially in Italy, during the 1960s and '70s. It is not far from *The Night Porter*, a serious-intentioned if uncomfortable film (featuring a skinny Charlotte Rampling, erotically dressed in Nazi uniform, performing a cabaret routine for SS guards), to garish exploitation fare such as Tinto Brass's *Salon Kitty* (1978), a voyeuristic sex film set in a Nazi-run brothel where women are forced to work as prostitutes and undergo all manner of degradation.

Since the 1970s film-makers in western Europe have resorted to more traditional and conservative forms. This is most evident in France, where, following the controversy over *Lacombe, Lucien*, the resistance narrative reverted to the valorization of individual heroism in films such as François Truffaut's *The Last Metro* (*Le dernier métro*, 1980) and Claude Berri's *Lucie Aubrac* (1997). The plight of Jewish victims of the Holocaust was examined in films such as Malle's *Au revoir, les enfants* (1987) and Agnieszka Holland's *Europa Europa* (1991). While these films make oblique reference to the tragedy of war, their focus is really on individual tales of courage and survival: historical process as autobiography. The popular success of Roberto Benigni's *Life is Beautiful* (*La vita è bella*, 1998), which became by far the highest grossing foreign-language film in North America ($58 million) and won Academy Awards for Best Foreign Film and Best Actor (Benigni), reawakened an ongoing debate over the cinematic representation of the Holocaust. In fact, it is hardly a war film at all. Much of the film is a slapstick comedy and it is only in the last third that the war intrudes when the main protagonist, Guido, a Jew, and his young son are imprisoned in a concentration camp. Guido devises a ruse to conceal the danger from Joshua by pretending that everyone in the camp is playing a game and that the prize will be a tank. It was this element of the film that attracted controversy. While some accepted it as a fable rather than a realistic account of life in a death camp, others averred that it trivialized the Holocaust by treating it as comedy. Even those who admired Benigni's comic talents – Philip French, for example, compared it to

Chaplin's *The Great Dictator* – thought that overall the film 'has a hollow, dispiriting ring'.[67]

The response to *Life is Beautiful* demonstrates the extent to which historical memory of the Holocaust remains extremely sensitive. The Holocaust has come to be regarded as the most uniquely dreadful of events: different from other historical genocides not merely by its scale but by the highly planned and organized method of its execution. Benigni was criticized not so much on grounds of taste but rather because he 'transgressed the usual artistic convention in depiction of the Holocaust – a certain grieving restraint'.[68] There are some who maintain that the Holocaust is so utterly impossible to comprehend that it is resistant to filming: this view seems to have informed some of the criticisms of *Life is Beautiful*. Others insist that the story must be told; but the problem for film-makers is how to tell it. In fact, the Holocaust has given rise to a wide array of different filmic interpretations. One mode is the 'factual' documentary that uses archive film to demonstrate precisely what happened in the death camps. The first example of this approach, a film compiled by Alfred Hitchcock and Stewart McAllister for SHAEF and intended for use in the 'de-Nazification' of Germany, was shelved for political reasons and never shown.[69] More recently, television series such as *The World at War* and *Auschwitz* have used archive film and eyewitness testimony to document the horrors of the camps. They are notable for their shocking imagery and moving testimony, but at the same time reveal the limitations of television (and for that matter film) narratives: they are better at showing 'how' than they are in explaining 'why'. In fact, there is a debate amongst historians between what have been called 'intentionalist' and 'structuralist' accounts of the Holocaust: these do not translate easily into a visual medium. Another approach is the exploration of the 'memory' of the Holocaust, whether this is done through archive film such as Alain Resnais's *Night and Fog* (*Nuit et brouillard*, 1956) or solely through oral testimony such as Claude Lanzmann's monumental *Shoah* (1985).

The most successful of all films about the Holocaust – at least if success is measured quantitatively – is Steven Spielberg's *Schindler's List* (1993). *Schindler's List* represents a synthesis of the different modes of representing the Holocaust: as both personal narrative and historical process, and as both authentic account (shot on location at Auschwitz) and an aestheticized treatment (monochrome with a few colour moments for heightened effect). Spielberg was criticized in some quarters for 'Hollywoodizing' the Holocaust: in focusing on the efforts of the Austrian businessman Oskar Schindler to save more than a thousand Jews from the death camps he transforms historical events into a linear structure with a redemptive ending. Others felt that he had 'written out' of the Holocaust those who were not fortunate enough to escape through the agency of Schindler. Ora Gelley, for example, argues that *Schindler's List* is compromised in so far as 'the perpetrators are the force which drives the film's aesthetic and narrative pleasure, while the victims stand unmoored, condemned to a silence which is invested with the entire burden of the incomprehensibility of the events of the Holocaust'.[70] This seems an unconvincing argument, especially given that the chief perpetrator of atrocities in the film, ss

Schindler's List (Steven Spielberg, 1993).

Commandant Goeth (a chilling performance by Ralph Fiennes), is a supporting character: the narrative is driven by Schindler (Liam Neeson) and his accountant Isaak Stern (Ben Kingsley). What *Schindler's List* documents is not just the cruelty of the Holocaust but also the humanity that was possible even in the midst of the most dreadful circumstances. In defence of Spielberg it should also be said that his reconstruction of daily life in Auschwitz, not least the arbitrariness of death, is probably the most authentic account of that most awful episode of the Second World War. The principal achievement of *Schindler's List*, however, for all its compromises to dramatic convention, is that it raised public awareness of the Holocaust to a greater degree than any other film.

hearts of darkness

I suggested in chapter One that the ideological project of *Saving Private Ryan* was to reclaim the Second World War as the 'good war' following a cycle of films about the American experience in Vietnam. It was in the 1980s that Vietnam became 'Hollywood's favourite war'.[71] There had been only one major film about Vietnam made during the war itself: *The Green Berets* (1968) was John Wayne's patriotic epic endorsing the role of the US military in the campaign against the Communist Vietcong. *The Green Berets* is unusual not so much for its overt propagandizing – to that extent it represents merely a reworking of the conventions of all the combat movies produced during the Second World War – but rather for the fact that its politics seem so fundamentally out of tune with the film industry in the late 1960s. This is usually seen as a period of liberalism in Hollywood when a combination of factors – including the decline of cinema audiences, corporate instability and the relaxation of censorship – permitted the production of films that, rather than appealing to the conserva- tive values of Middle America, responded to the emergence of counter-cultural movements with films about social alienation (*Easy Rider*, *Midnight Cowboy*) and violent self-destructive anti- heroes (*Bonnie and Clyde*, *The Wild Bunch*). In this context *The Green Berets* was an aberration. The fact that it was also a popu- lar aberration (it was a commercial success despite some derisive reviews) probably had as much to do with the enduring appeal of its star than with any reflection of public opinion about Vietnam.[72] Like many propaganda films, *The Green Berets* was overtaken by events: it was released after the Tet Offensive had dented the myth of American invincibility, while eighteen months later news of the My Lai massacre did irreparable damage to the image of the American military.

Apart from this one aberration, Hollywood's response to Vietnam was tardy. It may be that while the war was in progress it was too close to home for films to engage with and that therefore Vietnam was displaced onto other genres. Westerns such as *Soldier Blue* and *Little Big Man* have often been interpreted as Vietnam allegories, both films feature the massacre of Native Americans by the US Cavalry. The sense of moral confusion arising from Vietnam also informed two satirical black comedies set during the Second World War (*Catch 22*) and Korea (*M*A*S*H*). It was only after the last US troops had been withdrawn from Vietnam in 1975 that Hollywood felt able to address the war directly. *Go Tell the Spartans* (1978) and *Apocalypse Now* (1979) were the first Vietnam combat films, followed by *Missing in Action* (1984), *Rambo: First Blood Part II* (1985), *Platoon* (1986), *Hamburger Hill* (1987), *Full Metal Jacket* (1987), *Gardens of Stone* (1987), *Casualties of War* (1989) and *Born on the Fourth of July* (1989). The Vietnam cycle is less consistent in content and style than has sometimes been acknowledged. Ian McKellar identifies three distinct phases: the 'tale of moral confusion and the returning vet' in the late 1970s (*Apocalypse Now*, *The Deer Hunter*), the 'revenge film' in the early to mid-1980s (*Missing in Action*, *Rambo*) and the 'realistic combat film' later in the 1980s (*Platoon*, *Hamburger Hill*, *Full Metal Jacket*).[73] If we leave out the 'revenge' films (I will, however, return to *Rambo* in the next chapter), it is possible to identify a number of common themes and character-istics that link these films.

Except for *Apocalypse Now*, which demonstrates a level of stylistic excess so extreme that it can best be described as operatic (suitably so given its Wagnerian moments), Vietnam combat movies tended to be realistic in content. The critical reception of the films, indeed, recalls the vocabulary used in relation to the combat movies of the 1940s and '50s. Thus *Platoon* was described as 'brutal, vicious, surpassingly ugly – in a word [*sic*] realistic', while *Hamburger Hill* was 'the most realistic portrayal of the Viet-nam War ever filmed'.[74] These two films, in particular, were seen as being particularly realistic because they reflected 'true' experi-ences of Vietnam. Oliver Stone, director of *Platoon* (and *Born on the Fourth of July*), had served in Vietnam, as had James Carabat-sos, screenwriter of *Hamburger Hill*, while the latter film's director, John Irvin, had covered the war as a documentary film-maker. And *Full Metal Jacket* also aspired to a level of authenticity through its casting of a former drill sergeant, R. Lee Ermey, as the sadistic and foul-mouthed Gunnery Sergeant Hartman.

The other common theme between these films is the confusion of war: not just of the combat experience itself but also the moral confusion over American involvement in the war. *Apoc-alypse Now*, *Platoon* and *Hamburger Hill* all create a strong impression of the physical hardships of jungle warfare. The enemy remains unseen and mostly off-screen: the Vietcong sniper who pins down a whole platoon in *Full Metal Jacket* is finally revealed to be a teenage girl. There are familiar archetypes of anti-war cinema, including the wide-eyed innocent who arrives in the combat zone (*Platoon*) and the bullying sergeant (*Full Metal Jacket*). Perhaps the most significant feature of the Vietnam combat cycle, however, is that several of the films show American servicemen committing war crimes. *Apocalypse Now* includes scenes of the bombing and machine-gunning of a Vietcong village; *Platoon* features a sequence in which American soldiers, angered by the death of one of their comrades, terrorize a village, bludgeoning and shooting several of the inhabitants; *Casualties of War* revolves around the rape and murder of a Vietnamese girl by members of an American platoon. The films seem to attribute these atrocities to the madness of war. They suggest that participation in war erodes conscience and causes a descent into brutality and barbarism.

The Vietnam combat films also rework, possibly even subvert, the conventions of the Second World War combat movie. The narratives of Second World War films demonstrate unity

Platoon (Oliver Stone, 1990).

Apocalypse Now (1979).

between Americans to face the common enemy – a recurring device of the films is the social outsider who is assimilated into the unit – but the Vietnam films focus as much on conflicts within the unit as they do on the conflict with the enemy. This theme, evident not only in realistic combat films such as *Platoon* and *Casualties of War* but also in *Missing in Action*, reflects the divisive nature of the Vietnam War for American society: the films blame the failure of the war on the lack of a political consensus. The most schematic example of this is in *Platoon*, where the Americans are literally fighting amongst themselves: the 'good' sergeant Elias is shot by the 'bad' sergeant Barnes.

Another characteristic of the Vietnam cycle, like the films of the First World War, is that they seem to detach the war from its historical context. The main action of *Full Metal Jacket* is set against the background of the Tet Offensive of 1968 but this hardly matters; the other films could be set at almost any point

during the conflict. One critic wrote, for instance, that *Platoon* 'seems hermetically sealed off from history, taking place in a self-contained dramatic world'.[75] This sense of being outside history is accentuated by the loose narrative structures of the films, which are episodic and fragmentary: *Hamburger Hill* in particular consists of a sequence of 'contacts' that seem random and unlinked. What the films evoke is the atmosphere of war – its boredom, exhaustion, futility and horror – rather than any real sense of Vietnam as a historical experience.

The most ambitious of the Vietnam films was also the most pretentious. *Apocalypse Now* was produced at great expense ($30 million) by Francis Ford Coppola, who intended it as 'a film experience that would give its audience a sense of the horror, the madness, the sensuousness, and the moral dilemma of the Vietnam war'.[76] The narrative – in which Captain Willard (Martin Sheen) is sent 'to terminate with extreme prejudice' the renegade Colonel Kurtz (Marlon Brando), who is conducting his own private war deep in the jungle – was loosely based on Joseph Conrad's novella *Heart of Darkness* (1902) about a mercenary in the Belgian Congo, though the film has an epic and allegorical scope that belies its origin. Critics admired *Apocalypse Now* for its cinematography and its brilliant set pieces, most famously the helicopter attack, but felt that its narrative was too meandering and that its conclusion was incoherent (as indeed was Brando's mumbled dialogue). On one level, the fragmented and disjointed narrative reflects the film's troubled production history: the Philippine locations were disrupted by a hurricane and by the haphazard provision of military hardware by the Philippine government. On another level, however, the unstructured narrative can be seen as a means of representing the confusion and chaos of a war that lacks a clear sense of moral purpose. Willard's journey up river meanders from one incident to the next: it is a series of unconnected episodes rather than a linear progression.

It has even been argued that Willard's journey is a dream: the opening sequence with its highly subjective camerawork and Willard's dazed voice-over narration suggests that what follows may be a hallucinatory experience.[77] *Apocalypse Now* is better understood as a metaphorical or allegorical narrative rather than a realist film. This perhaps accounts for its mixed critical reception.

If *Apocalypse Now* was the first of the major Vietnam combat films, then *Full Metal Jacket* represents the apotheosis of the genre. It was produced later in the cycle (1987), when, as Thomas Doherty puts it, the Vietnam War film had reached 'its mature stage'.[78] Stanley Kubrick had already made one of the best First World War films, *Paths of Glory*; *Full Metal Jacket* is another powerful indictment of the futility of war and the in-humanity of militarism. In contrast to Coppola's bloated and meandering epic, Kubrick's film is austere and tightly controlled, exhibiting its director's customary clinical attention to detail. The choreography of the action sequences is breathtaking and the climax, in which a lone sniper decimates an entire squad of bewildered US Marines, anticipates *Saving Private Ryan* in its highly realistic representation of the physical trauma of combat. What particularly distinguishes *Full Metal Jacket*, however, is that it examines not only the war itself but also the process of training and indoctrination that turns men into killers. The first third of the film is set at the US Marine boot camp at Parris Island, South Carolina, where a group of new recruits are subject to the brutal training regime of Sergeant Hartman, whose methods include both verbal and physical abuse. The film draws a parallel between military training and ideological indoctrination: the recruits are taught to love their rifles and hate the enemy. One recruit, the overweight 'Private Pyle' (Hartman renames all the recruits according to his whim), is victimized for his failure to meet the physical demands of training and is bullied by the others when they are punished for his shortcomings. Pyle eventually begins to respond to training as a virtual zombie: he fetishizes his rifle and eventually uses it to kill Hartman and then himself. Whereas other films such as *The Way Ahead* and *Heartbreak Ridge* represent military training as rigorous but fair and focus on its team-building ethos, *Full Metal Jacket* suggests that it is even more brutalizing and dehumanizing than combat itself.

If *Full Metal Jacket* is a more complete and satisfying representation of the Vietnam experience than *Apocalypse Now* it is not because it is necessarily any more authentic. Nor is it any more linear in its structure: its narrative is similarly episodic once the Marines have arrived in the combat zone. What particularly distinguishes *Full Metal Jacket* is its ironic detachment from its subject: the film is very much aware of its status as a film. Kubrick does not provide the massive visual spectacle of Coppola but rather comments on the mediated nature of images of war through the device of a film crew who interview soldiers on camera for 'Vietnam – The Movie'. The official view of the war is represented by the patriotic armed forces magazine *Stars and Stripes*, for which Private Joker, the only character carried forward from the training sequence, is now a reporter. Joker, whose intellect sets him apart both from the other 'grunts' and from the military hierarchy, is fully aware of the absurdity of war: he wears a CND badge on his flak jacket while his helmet bears the

Full Metal Jacket (Stanley Kubrick, 1987).

legend 'Born to kill'. When reprimanded by an officer for this apparent contradiction, Joker replies: 'I think I was trying to say something about the duality of man . . . The Jungian thing, sir.'

Rich Schweitzer asserts that '*Full Metal Jacket* argues for an historical understanding of Vietnam which places the violence of the war squarely within an American context'.[79] In this reading the film 'explains' American involvement in Vietnam through references to the myth of the frontier (Private Joker impersonating John Wayne) and through a doctrine of US cultural and political imperialism ('We are here to help the Vietnamese because inside every gook there's an American trying to get out'). Doherty advances a counter argument that the film represents Vietnam as a 'cinematic, not historical, experience . . . a cinematic usurpation of the historical record that reaffirms the vital cultural function of genre'.[80] In this reading the film creates meaning not through what it says about Vietnam but rather through its references to other combat films, including *Sands of Iwo Jima* and *The Story of GI Joe*. It seems to me that both arguments have some substance: *Full Metal Jacket* is both an account of the American experience in Vietnam and a critical deconstruction of the combat film. And as such it represents perhaps the most complete filmic statement of the brutality, absurdity and confusion of the first war that America lost. Whether the current situation in Iraq will indeed turn out to be 'another Vietnam', as some political commentators have suggested, remains to be seen. The outcome of the war will surely determine its filmic representation: Hollywood, as it always has done, will respond to the ideological and cultural imperatives of the present when it comes to providing a filmic historiography of America's wars.

3 war as adventure

rehabilitating rambo

The major Hollywood 'event' movie of 1985 was *Rambo: First Blood Part II*, the first sequel to the 1982 film *First Blood*. *First Blood*, based on a novel by David Morrell, was about a Vietnam veteran who is set upon by the local police chief when he arrives at a small town in the Pacific Rockies for no better reason than having long hair. John Rambo, who turns out to be a former Green Beret with Special Forces training, is abused in jail – triggering memories of his torture at the hands of the Vietcong – and subsequently escapes into the mountains with the National Guard in pursuit. Rambo puts his survivalist skills and military training to good use in evading his pursuers and leaves a trail of destruction in his wake. *First Blood* was an entry in a cycle of films examining the alienation and social exclusion of Vietnam veterans unable to adjust to a society that had turned its backs on them: other examples included *The Deer Hunter* (1978), *Coming Home* (1978) and, later, *Born on the Fourth of July* (1989). Its commercial success (a domestic box-office gross of $57 million) was sufficient to prompt a sequel. *Rambo: First Blood Part II* is in fact one of the few sequels that is more than a remake of the first film. It switches genres from the maladjusted veteran drama to the MIA ('Missing in Action') movie, though, again, it followed on the

Rambo: First Blood Part II (George Pan Cosmatos, 1985).

heels of other films such as *Uncommon Valor* (1983) and *Missing in Action* (1984) rather than being a trailblazer in its own right. What was particularly significant about *Rambo*, however, was that it far exceeded its predecessor at the box office, grossing $150 million – an achievement no doubt helped by the fact that it 'opened' on 2,074 screens and was supported by a massive promotional campaign by its independent producer-distributor, Carolco. A wave of 'Rambomania' swept the United States with merchandise

ranging from Rambo action dolls to authentic replicas of his arsenal of weapons, including bow and arrow and a deadly serrated-edged hunting knife.[1]

The story of *Rambo*, co-written by its star Sylvester Stallone and *Terminator* director James Cameron, is a classically structured mission-adventure narrative. Rambo, serving a term in prison after the events of the first film, is released into the custody of his former commanding officer Colonel Trautman, who offers him a pardon in return for Rambo undertaking a covert mission: to return to Vietnam to establish whether missing servicemen are still being held in captivity. Rambo parachutes into Vietnam and travels upriver with his Vietnamese guide, Co Bao. He discovers that there are indeed American prisoners being held in atrocious conditions. Rambo rescues one of them – his instructions had been only to return with photographic evidence – and returns to the rendezvous point. At this point the helicopter sent to retrieve him is aborted on the orders of Murdock, the

US government official in charge of the operation. Rambo is captured and taken back to the camp, where he is tortured by the Vietcong and their Russian 'advisers'. With the help of Co Bao, who sneaks into the camp disguised as a prostitute, Rambo escapes and inflicts heavy casualties on his pursuers. Co Bao is killed; Rambo commandeers a helicopter and returns to the camp to rescue the rest of the prisoners. It transpires that the mission had been a political exercise to prove there were no 'MIAs' in Vietnam: their existence is an embarrassment for the government. Rambo shoots up the command base and warns Murdock to find the other prisoners – or else.

The critical reception of *Rambo* was divided between those who dismissed it as crass exploitation and those who responded to its deeper ideological undertones. The trade paper *Variety* derided its 'risible production [and] comic book heroics'.[2] David Denby thought it 'a goofy piece of right-wing erotic exploitation'.[3] Vincent Canby similarly found it 'implausible if not truly bubble-headed' and described Stallone's pumped-up performance as 'something of a camp classic'.[4] Pauline Kael called it 'overwrought' and 'a wired-up version of the narcissistic jingoism of the John Wayne–Second World War pictures'.[5] For J. Hoberman it was 'crudely schematic . . . a revenge fantasy tailored to the age of Reagan'.[6] In Britain, where the film was also a tremendous box-office success, the reception focused more on its violence: there were campaigns to ban it in some towns.[7] It was predictable, perhaps, that the communist *Morning Star* would condemn it as a 'bloodthirsty reactionary film'.[8] But this view was also shared by others. Alexander Walker wrote that 'the body culture he [Stallone] goes in for is as nauseating as the body-count he precipitates' and added for good measure that 'I'd hate to belong to a society that produced this monster.'[9] Francis Wheen found himself unable to write it off as simple-minded escapism: 'The sight of Rambo single-handedly wiping out hundreds of Vietnamese troops without sustaining an injury would be so preposterous as to be laughable, if it weren't for the fact that most viewers are likely to take it seriously.'[10] Adam Mars-Jones, similarly, felt that the film's popularity must appeal to baser human instincts: 'The utter crudity of *Rambo* as propaganda is worrying in itself. Since the film has no prospect of convincing anyone of anything, it must be relying on reflexes that are already there.' 'An audience that enjoys *Rambo*', he added, 'in spite of its pitiful failures as an action film, must be like the audience of a sex film, willing to tolerate any discontinuity as long as the desired deeds are done often enough.'[11]

Rambo has come to symbolize everything that was critically abused and ideologically irredeemable about American cinema of the 1980s. Its combination of violent action and *über-patriotic* sentiments were the hallmark of what came to be dubbed 'Reaganite' cinema after the personality and policies of the former Hollywood actor who occupied the White House for most of the decade. Ronald Reagan's presidency was characterized by an assertive foreign policy – including military interventions in Grenada and Nicaragua – and by domestic social and economic policies that championed self-assertiveness and the aggressive pursuit of personal ambition. The new confidence and assertiveness of American cinema during the Reagan presidency is evident in militaristic films such as *Top Gun*, *Iron Eagle* and *Heartbreak Ridge* (all 1986) and in the cycle of anti-communist propaganda films including *Firefox* (1982), *Red Dawn* (1984) and *Rocky IV* (1985). *Rambo* soon came to represent the apotheosis of what Andrew Britton called 'the politics of Reaganite entertainment'.[12] The character of Rambo even entered into Reaganite political discourse when, during the Beirut hostage crisis in 1985, the president revealed himself as a fan of the film when he remarked: 'After seeing *Rambo* last night I know what to do the next time this happens.'[13] (The remark was captured by an open microphone and may have been, like Reagan's infamous 'We start bombing in five minutes', an off-the-cuff remark that he may or may not have intended for public consumption. However, it was not the only occasion on which Reagan referred to the film, once, for example, telling a group of assembled journalists: 'In the spirit of Rambo, let me tell you – we're gonna win this time.')[14]

'Do we get to win this time?' is Rambo's question when his commanding officer asks him to return to Vietnam. The politics of *Rambo* – the film is political without necessarily being a political film – are related to revisionist interpretations of the Vietnam War. Reagan's campaign for the White House in 1980 had been notable in so far as he had challenged the conventional view that the war had been meaningless: he referred to it as a 'noble cause' and argued that it had been lost not by the military but by the failure of politicians in Washington who had been 'afraid to win'.[15] To an extent, of course, this was politically expedient, since he wanted to win the veterans' vote, but it also signalled a shift in popular attitudes towards the war and its conduct that included the rehabilitation of the veteran. *First Blood* had endorsed a Reaganite interpretation of the war when Rambo says 'I did what I had to do to win. But somebody wouldn't let us win.' *Rambo* suggests even more stridently that it was politicians who lost the war because they did not have the will to prosecute it vigorously and subsequently laid the blame on the military. The conclusion of *Rambo* makes an unequivocal plea for the rehabilitation of the Vietnam veteran: 'I want what they want and what every other guy who came over here and spilt his guts and gave everything he had wants: for our country to love us as much as we love it.'

The revisionist politics of *Rambo* are mapped onto an issue that Reagan himself had declared in 1983 to be a matter of 'the highest national priority'.[16] There were still a total of 2,477 American servicemen officially listed as 'missing in action'. Many Americans, particularly relatives of the MIAs, clung to the belief that they were not dead but were still prisoners. Stallone averred that he was moved to make *Rambo* when he received a letter from a Virginian woman who believed her husband had been held captive for sixteen years: 'It got to me. I'm convinced that the MIAs are alive. Living in Laos. There's been a great avoidance of the issue. The country has been shoving it under the mat and forgetting it.'[17] No matter that the Pentagon had declared in 1978 that there were no American prisoners in Vietnam, nor that all reliable evidence suggests that the 'MIA myth' is precisely that, *Rambo* nevertheless supports the notion of Americans in captivity and, moreover, being abused and maltreated by their brutal and sadistic captors. In fact, it is the existence of the MIAs that the narrative of *Rambo* employs as justification for American intervention in

Southeast Asia. It is an occasion where the myth – what people believe – is more potent than the reality.[18]

That said, however, critics felt that the employment of the MIA myth in *Rambo* was at worst exploitative and at best superficial. Richard Shickel attacked *Rambo* and other MIA films such as *Uncommon Valor* and *Missing in Action* for their 'superficial references to dangerous, live moral issues'. He argued that these films 'exploit and travesty emotions that a decent movie would try to help us share more deeply'.[19] Vincent Canby similarly felt that the film was

> almost as opportunistic as the Congressman it pretends to abhor. In spite of everything it says, it's much less interested in the MIA question than it is in finding a topical frame for the kind of action-adventure in which Mr Stallone – his torso and his vacant stare – can do what his fans like best. That is fight, outwit and kill, usually all by himself, dozens of far better armed but lesser mortals.[20]

It seems to me that, unless we assume that all audiences were right-wing revisionists, the pleasures of *Rambo* are mainly to be derived from factors other than its politics. In this context, indeed, it should be remembered that the film was popular not only in America but in other territories too, including, bizarrely, in Syria, where it was dubbed in such a way as to turn the Vietcong into Japanese and Vietnam into Burma during the Second World War.[21] It is symptomatic of the intellectual disdain for what might be termed 'the cinema of the right' that the aesthetic

Rambo: First Blood Part II.

qualities of a film such as *Rambo* have been largely overlooked. Yet *Rambo* is, in large measure, a very classical film: its narrative – a taut, spare, economical 92 minutes – conforms much closer to the classical model than the bloated, meandering *Apocalypse Now*, which is so often claimed as one of the greatest war movies. *Rambo* is also a very attractively photographed film, no doubt attributable to the veteran British cinematographer Jack Cardiff. Kael remarked that Cardiff 'gets something of the effect in color that Josef von Sternberg got in black-and-white in a studio-made jungle in his 1953 *Anatahan* – it's is as if every leaf has been oiled and buffed'.[22] And, on a more basic level perhaps, *Rambo* exemplifies the sort of visual pyrotechnics – it is replete with Big Orange Explosions – that characterize the genre.

The principal spectacle in *Rambo*, however, is not its action set pieces, no matter how impressively they are choreographed, but its star. Stallone, who came to stardom by writing and starring in *Rocky*, is representative of a generation of American leading men whose mode of performance is based almost entirely on the display of the male body. Yvonne Tasker has observed that *Rambo* 'signalled a new visibility for the muscular hero of the action cinema'.[23] *Rambo* misses no opportunity to showcase its star's body: Stallone, like his contemporaries Arnold Schwarzenegger and Jean-Claude Van Damme, acts principally with his biceps and pectorals. The heavily muscular male body, pumped up to exaggerated proportions, becomes a potent symbol of masculinity and strength as well as an object of spectacle.

The spectacle of Stallone's body in *Rambo* is open to different readings. On the one hand the association between physical culture and violence is redolent of Fascism. This is a reading that reinforces a view of *Rambo* and other films of its ilk as ideologically pernicious. Jeffrey Richards, for example, groups Rambo with other popular icons of 1980s cinema such as Mel Gibson's Mad Max and Arnold Schwarzenegger's Conan the Barbarian, seeing them as representing a decisive shift away from the culture of chivalry associated with the classical swashbuckling heroes of the screen such as Robin Hood, Tarzan and The Scarlet Pimpernel. In contrast Rambo, Mad Max and Conan represent

> the glorification of violence, an emphasis on fighting as the definition of masculinity, the rejection of chivalry and the triumph of the individual will . . . Schwarzenegger and Stallone resemble nothing so much as the absurdly over-muscled, bulging thewed male statues produced by Arno Breker and Dr Josef Thorak, the favourite sculptors of the [Third] Reich.[24]

Rambo: First Blood Part II.

On the other hand, however, the camera's fetishization of the body has opened up these films to interpretation as a form of homoerotic spectacle. This was a reading advanced at the time by *The Spectator* critic Peter Ackroyd, who suggested that 'in *Rambo* the cult of the body beautiful is wholly for the benefit of the male sex, who can apparently admire all those biceps and triceps without impugning their own sexuality'.[25] *Rambo* is replete with scenes in which Stallone, stripped to the waist, stretches the sinews of his body, whether he is spread-eagled on a rack by his sadistic captors (a scene recalling the flogging in *Lawrence of Arabia* with its decidedly homoerotic overtones) or brandishing with one hand massively phallic weaponry such as a belt-fed machine gun or rocket launcher.

It seems to me, however, that the success of *Rambo* is due mainly to the pleasures of the action-adventure movie. There is a sense that, for all its contemporary political resonance, *Rambo* is nothing more or less than a traditional adventure film. Janet

Maslin, for one, saw in it 'a sweeping action movie of the sort that has all but gone out of style . . . The conventions of *Rambo*, for all the plot's supposed topicality, could apply as well to a Biblical epic or a western.'[26] It belongs to a lineage of action-adventure films that also includes the likes of *The Last of the Mohicans*, *Gunga Din*, *The Vikings* and *The Professionals*. I am making no claim that *Rambo* is in the same bracket as those films in terms of quality, but it is an heir to the same tradition. Rambo himself is nothing if not a late twentieth-century version of the frontier scout 'Hawkeye' in James Fenimore Cooper's Leatherstocking tales. Like Hawkeye, an Englishman who has gone native, Rambo is a 'noble savage': his long hair and ethnicity (he is established as being of Indian/German descent) associate him with nature-in-the-raw. It is significant in this regard that, despite all the high-tech weaponry at his disposal, Rambo's weapons of choice are his hunting knife and bow (though his arrows have explosive heads). It is ironic that in the film Rambo triumphs through his mastery of the sort of guerrilla tactics that the Vietcong had adopted against technologically superior US forces during the Vietnam War itself. *Rambo* is a variation on *The Last of the Mohicans* (filmed with Randolph Scott in 1936 and again with Daniel Day Lewis in 1992) in which Rambo assumes the role of a scout who rescues the captive whites and escorts them to safety through a hostile environment.

It has been argued that the visual iconography of *Rambo* makes conscious allegorical references. In the scene of Rambo being tortured by the Russian colonel (for which Stephen Berkoff repeats his manic twitching-eyed performance from the James

Bond film *Octopussy*) he is bound in what to all intents and purposes is the Crucifixion position: electric shocks and a red-hot knife against the cheek replace the crown of thorns and the nails through the hands. Rambo's flowing hair has even prompted parallels with the myth of Samson: both are great warriors who become deliverers of their people. The plight of Samson in Milton's 'Samson Agonistes' – that he delivers the Israelites 'from Philistine yoke' only to be cast out himself – is reflected in the character of Rambo. Just as Samson pulled down the temple, at the end of the film Rambo turns his M-60 on the army command headquarters 'and blasts the machinery of a bureaucracy that has failed him once again'.[27]

This may be making exaggerated claims for what is, essentially, no more and no less than an action movie. Yet judged purely as an action movie Rambo is no worse than others of its kind. In particular, the hysterical reaction to its extreme violence seems misplaced. Rambo may be characterized as a 'pure fighting machine' but the body count in the film is less than in *Where Eagles Dare* or even some of the James Bond films: he does not slay 'hundreds of Vietnamese troops' as so often averred, but several dozen. One critic averred that '*Rambo*'s violence is staged with a not unsatisfying balletic quality' reminiscent of the spaghetti westerns of the 1960s.[28] The violence that Rambo inflicts is both sanitized (none of the shooting, stabbing or garrotting is especially gruesome: the film is far removed from the visual realism of *Saving Private Ryan*) and, in the narrative context of the film at least, morally justified: those whom he kills have tortured him and others. The most overblown death (literally) is the Vietcong officer who has shot and killed Co Bao: his fate (blown to smithereens by one of Rambo's explosive-tipped arrows) seems fitting retribution. Indeed, for all the charges levelled against *Rambo* for its excessive and overblown narrative, the film seems quite economical and even restrained. *Rambo* is a classical action adventure movie and offers the pleasures associated with that genre: the failure of *Rambo III* (which sent our hero on another special mission, this time to Soviet-occupied Afghanistan) to match its popular success demonstrates how elusive those pleasures can be.

the pleasure culture of war

Rambo belongs to a tradition of popular cinema that exemplifies what, following Graham Dawson, we may term 'the pleasure-culture of war'.[29] Historians have come to recognize only recently the extent to which mass popular culture has been employed for projecting images that, far from suggesting 'war is hell', seem positively to valorize it. Michael Paris, for example, has described the emergence of a pleasure culture of war in British juvenile fiction from the mid-nineteenth century, demonstrating how story papers such as *Boy's Own Paper*, *Union Jack*, *Young England*, *Pluck* and *Chums* and novelists such as R. M. Ballantyne, G. A. Henty and F. S. Brereton portrayed a heroic ideal of war as a noble and chivalrous enterprise. Their tales of heroism, derring-do and muscular Christianity 'created powerful myths about the nature of war and the British soldier'.[30] We might have expected the grim reality of the Western Front to mark the end of the pleasure culture of war, but if anything it was strengthened as the purveyors of juvenile fiction sought to come to terms with the great losses suffered by suggesting that the sacrifices had not been in vain and that the war had been fought for a just cause. It is testimony to how deep-rooted the codes of patriotism and duty had become that they survived the carnage of the Somme and Passchendaele and remained intact at a time when intellectual opinion was more receptive to the anti-war literature of Owen, Sassoon and Graves. The emergence of cinema as the foremost medium of popular entertainment around the time of the First World War brought visual images of war to an even wider public.

How can we account for the existence of this pleasure culture of war? Marxists would argue that popular culture, as an instrument of hegemony, is a vehicle through which ruling elites set out to indoctrinate the masses with the mentality necessary for the perpetuation of the warfare state. In this interpretation 'they' are preparing 'us' to fight 'their' wars. As we will see, there are historical examples of societies where this argument holds much currency, and not merely in totalitarian states: liberal democracies have also found it expedient at times to mobilize their populations for war. A counter argument would be that, rather than indoctrinating us, popular culture is merely reflecting back our fascination with war. There is probably not a society in which children have not played at being soldiers and in so doing have, as Joanna Bourke puts it, 'created narratives of pleasure around acts of killing'.[31] Popular hobbies such as collecting toy soldiers and constructing models of battleships, tanks and aeroplanes demonstrate fascination with the apparatus and machinery of war. Nor is war as a leisure activity confined to juveniles: the emergence of the 'adult' computer game based on the detailed visualization of the Second World War battlefield (*Code of Honour*, *Call of Duty*) and the simulation of combat in activities such as paint-balling are merely extensions of the games we played as children. At a time when few of us have the opportunity to participate in real war, it seems that we are increasingly obsessed with playing at war.

The pleasure culture of war probably reached its zenith during the first half of the twentieth century. This was also the period when cinema was at its height both as a medium of popular entertainment and as an instrument of propaganda and social control. While states such as Nazi Germany and Soviet Russia were amongst the first to realize the full potential of film propaganda, the liberal democracies were not far behind them, especially in the years immediately preceding as well as during the Second World War. Here I will focus on the promotion of the pleasure culture of war in British and German cinema, partly because these are two of the best-documented examples but also because they demonstrate that similar narratives of patriotism and duty were shared between two very different political cultures.

The cinema quickly assimilated the narrative conventions of popular war literature. The titles of films such as *Saving the Colours* (1914) and *His Country's Bidding* (1915) are indicative of their patriotic content. These films can be seen within the context of the film industry 'doing its duty' by promoting support for the British war effort. Perhaps the nearest equivalent to the tradition of juvenile fiction was *The Warrior Strain* (1919), in which the young son of an aristocratic family joins the cadet corps and proves his leadership qualities not only by standing up against the school bully but also by foiling a German spy conspiracy. It is an indication of a level of official support for this 45-minute feature that it includes an appearance by Edward, Prince of Wales, who decorates the boy-hero. It has sometimes been suggested that the war narrative marginalizes women and focuses solely on male heroism, though Hollywood 'serial queen' melodramas such as *The Secret of the Submarine* and *Pearl of the Army* (both 1916) – early examples of 'war preparedness' narratives – demonstrate that this is not always the case. The major Hollywood war films of the 1920s such as *The Big Parade* and *Wings*, for all their anti-war sentiments, focused on the camaraderie of the services and valorized an ideal of heroic masculinity.

The ideological project of British cinema throughout the 1930s was the promotion of a 'cinema of consensus'.[32] This was enforced by the policies of the British Board of Film Censors which frowned upon controversial subject matter (such as politics) and endorsed the cherished institutions of state and society including the monarchy, the church and the armed services. There is much evidence to suggest that the promotion of the pleasure culture of war was officially sanctioned. In the mid-1930s, for example, the Gaumont British Picture Corporation made two films that to all intents and purposes were recruiting vehicles for the armed services. *Forever England* (1935) was based on C. S. Forester's First World War adventure *Brown on Resolution* and starred a young John Mills as naval rating Albert Brown, who, wounded, alone and armed with only a rifle, pins down the crew of a damaged German cruiser in the Pacific until the arrival of a Royal Navy squadron to finish her off. Director Walter Forde averred that the Admiralty were 'unusually co-operative' in the production of the film, even providing four ships, including the battleship HMS *Iron Duke*.[33] The patriotic intent of the film was evident in the trailer, which described *Forever England* as 'a sea drama that will stir the blood of everyone of British stock'; the trade paper *Kinematograph Weekly* agreed that it was 'an inspiring tale of individual heroism and courage during the Great War, which finds its lofty, unforgettable theme in the true maxim, "Breed will tell"'.[34] The film, characteristic of British cinema of the period, endorses the class system. Albert Brown is the illegitimate son of an upper-class naval officer and a grocer's daughter (played by silent film star Betty Balfour, only five years older than her screen 'son' Mills) who accepts that she cannot marry her lover because of the difference in their social background. Brown dies from his wounds on Resolution Island but his father learns of his identity when he recognizes a watch, which he had given to Brown's mother and which she had passed on to her son, amongst Brown's effects. The idea of a natural 'warrior class' was shared between this film and other British films of the First World War, such as *Journey's End* and *Tell England*.

Gaumont British followed *Forever England* with *O.H.M.S.* (1936), which similarly was produced with the cooperation of the War Office and can be seen as a virtual recruiting film for the British Army. In what seems a deliberate strategy to appeal to the US market, the film follows the adventures of a small-time American racketeer (Wallace Ford) who flees to Britain and enlists in the 1st Wessex Regiment. The social politics are more egalitarian than in *Forever England* – again perhaps a sop to American tastes – though the outcome is largely the same, since the protagonist dies a redemptive heroic death in a campaign against bandits in China. The film is briskly directed by Raoul Walsh, an American director noted for his action movies. It was a popular success according to the journal *World Film News*: 'Propaganda is usually of doubtful box-office value, but in this case the trade considers that propaganda and entertainment have been admirably blended and look forward with confidence to a financial success.'[35] It was successful enough that it was virtually remade in Hollywood as *The Real Glory* (1939), in which soldiers of fortune Gary Cooper and David Niven joined the US Army and fought in the Philippines. Perhaps the main significance of *O.H.M.S.*, however, is that it provided the narrative template for a cycle of 'Yanks in Britain' propaganda films during the Second World War (*Eagle Squadron*, *International Squadron*, *A Yank in the RAF*), in which brash Americans and reserved Englishmen find they are really not so different after all.

O.H.M.S. can also be seen in the context of a cycle of imperial adventure films made in the later 1930s both in Britain (*King Solomon's Mines*, *The Drum*, *The Four Feathers*) and in Hollywood (*Lives of a Bengal Lancer*, *The Charge of the Light Brigade*, *Wee Willie Winkie*, *Gunga Din*). The emergence of this cycle at this time can be explained through the congruence of 'patriotism with profit': the films were promoting an ideology of popular imperialism while also providing the combination of narrative excitement and exotic spectacle that scored at the box office.[36]

The films demonstrate once again the links between cinema and popular literature, including adaptations of Sir Henry Rider Haggard (*King Solomon's Mines*), A.E.W. Mason (*The Drum*, *The Four Feathers*) and Rudyard Kipling (*Wee Willie Winkie*, *Gunga Din*). They imagine the British Empire as a site of adventure and heroism and the army as an instrument for preserving peace and protecting millions of people from native tyrants and despots. It is significant here that Warner Bros. reinterpreted one of Britain's greatest military disasters as a heroic saga of retribution, in which the Charge of the Light Brigade is a deliberately suicidal action undertaken to destroy a cruel Indian potentate (at the Battle of Balaclava!). The imperial films also promote a rigid social structure through the idea of a warrior elite who have historically served nation and empire. The protagonists of *The Charge of the Light Brigade* ('The Vickers are an old army family. I knew your father at Sandhurst') and *The Four Feathers* ('First time for a hundred years there hasn't been a Faversham in the army and look at the mess they make!') are both the inheritors of a tradition of military service. The themes of patriotism, duty and *noblesse oblige* hark back to the popular imperialism of the nineteenth century.

The production of films that presented war as a heroic spectacle can be seen as part of a process of ideological realignment within popular cinema as it sought to distance itself from the anti-war films of the early 1930s and prepare its public for the possibility of another major war. Nowhere was this realignment process better demonstrated than in German cinema during the Third Reich, where anti-war films such as *Westfront 1918* and *The*

The Four Feathers
(Zoltan Korda,
1939)

Other Side were banned and the film industry turned its efforts to promoting a much more positive representation of war and the military image. In fact, as Rainer Rother has demonstrated, this process can be seen to have begun towards the end of the Weimar Republic when films such as *Douaumont* and *Tannenberg* 'lend themselves to a heroic interpretation of the War'.[37] The process accelerated after 1933 as a consequence of the Nazi project to 'correct' the image of the First World War from the pacifist sentiments of films like *All Quiet on the Western Front*. There was a cycle of films about the First World War – *Shock Troop 1917* (*Strosstrupp 1917*, 1934), *Drumfire of the Western Front* (*Trommelfeuer der Westfront*, 1936), *The Michael Action* (*Unternehmen Michael*, 1937) and *Thirteen Men and a Cannon* (*Dreizehn Mann und eine Kanone*, 1938) – that eulogized the heroism of German soldiers. These films focused on themes of comradeship, honour and duty. The experience of the war was presented not as a senseless sacrifice but as a test of courage and strength 'through which emerges a new type of human being – hardened by the "storm of steel"'.[38] Joseph Goebbels, the Reich Propaganda Minister, was keen that films should not be too overtly propagandistic in content. He disliked the more didactic *Shoulder Arms* (*Das Gewehr über*, 1939) – about a German settler from Australia who returns home reluctantly for military service – because it was 'a bad Wehrmacht propaganda film. Came close to a ban.'[39]

The themes of German war films during the Third Reich – comradeship, masculinity, patriotism and a sentimental belief in home and nation – are in fact not significantly different from their counterparts in British films. A cycle of films about the Hitler Youth – including *Chin Up, Johannes* (*Kopf hoch, Johannes!*, 1940), *Cadets* (*Kadetten*, 1941) and *Bloody Dogs* (*Himmelhunde*, 1942) – were part of a programme to prepare the nation's youth for military service, but their narrative conventions are not fundamentally different from *The Warrior Strain* or *Forever England*. One of the most popular films of the war was *Quax the Test Pilot* (*Quax, der Bruchpilot*, 1941), starring Heinz Rühmann as a young travel clerk who wins free flying lessons. He is afraid of flying and disguises this through mock bravado, which leads to his expulsion from flying school, but he earns a second chance and proves himself. The narrative of *Quax* is essentially about the emergence of manhood as the protagonist matures from a juvenile to a responsible adult: to this extent it represents a theme of Nazi cinema in which the 'primary objective [is] the reformation of the outsider or deviant male lead'.[40] The character of Quax is perhaps best described as a sort of German Biggles: indeed, the sequel, *Quax in Africa* (1945), is very much in the spirit of W. E. Johns. It is only the nationality of the protagonist that is different. The promotion of the aviator as a heroic archetype and the presentation of the Africans as primitive and superstitious are common to both.

The aviation film was a particularly appropriate vehicle for representing the pleasure culture of war. The genre offers more scope for individual heroism than army or navy films that focus on the heterogeneous military unit: in an age of increasingly mechanized warfare the aviator remains an individual warrior whose success is determined by courage and skill. The 1930s had seen cycles of aviation films in Germany (*Rivals of the Air*, *Pour le Mérite*, *D I 1188*), Italy (*Cavalleria*, *The Last Roll Call*) and the USSR (*Flyers*, *The Motherland Calls*, *Number Five Squadron*). Aviation themes were seen as an assertion of technological prowess and modernity: for this reason they were particularly significant in those totalitarian cinemas that sought to project their societies as progressive and modern.[41] Mussolini and Goering were both former aviators; this is one reason why the aviator held a special place in Fascist cultures. The theme of the war in the air as an arena for heroism and adventure was explored in Second World War films such as *Stukas* (1941) and *Squadron Leader Lützow* (*Kampfgeschwader Lützow*, 1941). These films, and Hollywood counterparts such as *A Yank in the RAF* (1942), portrayed aerial warfare as glamorous and exciting. There is also the possibility of a heroic and redemptive death. The British film *Ships With Wings*, for example, climaxes with its disgraced hero redeeming himself in combat when he deliberately collides with a German

The Star of Africa
(Alfred Weidenmann,
1957).

bomber that is targeting the British flagship. *Ships With Wings* was derided for its melodramatic heroics in contrast to the realist aesthetic emerging in British cinema at the time: unrealistic it may have been, but it was a significant popular success.[42]

The archetype of the aviator hero persisted into the post-war period when films were made about the exploits of real-life war heroes. *Reach for the Sky* (1956) was a biopic of the British aviator Douglas Bader who lost his legs in a flying accident in the 1930s but returned to lead a Hurricane squadron during the Battle of Britain before being shot down over France in 1941 and spending the rest of the war as a prisoner. The film, based on a hagiography by Paul Brickhill, characterizes Bader (played in his best 'good chap' persona by Kenneth More) as a born warrior who overcomes his disability through sheer determination and then enjoys a distinguished war record. An opening caption summarizes the film's representation of Bader as an inspirational role model: 'Douglas Bader has become a legend in his own life time.

His courage was not only an example to those in War but is now a source of inspiration to many in Peace'. *Reach for the Sky* is a tale of individual heroism that whitewashes its protagonist: it barely even censures Bader for the accident that causes his crippling injuries and probably exaggerates his reputation as a fighter 'ace'. A similar whitewash takes place in *The Star of Africa* (*Der Stern von Afrika*, 1957) about the Luftwaffe fighter ace Hans Joachim Marseille (played by Joachim Hansen, the acceptable face of wartime heroics in West German cinema). The film ignores the inconvenient fact that Marseille was a fervent Nazi and character-izes him instead as a rebel who runs into trouble with his super-iors. Early in the film, for instance, he is told: 'It would be better if you thought less and followed orders.' This would seem a direct reference to a moment in *Quax, der Bruchpilot* where the hero is told 'Better that you shouldn't think!' by his instructor when he

Reach for the Sky (Lewis Gilbert, 1956).

starts to say 'I just thought . . .'. This highlights the different ideo-logical projects of the two films. Whereas in the Nazi-produced film discipline is seen as a good thing and the protagonist learns to conform, in the post-war film the hero's defiance and anti-author-itarian streak establish him as being apart from the regime.

The social and cultural politics of post-war films are significantly different from their predecessors. During the war the progressive *Documentary News Letter* had complained that *Convoy* – a naval drama that was the most successful British film at the box office in 1940 – 'managed to give the impression that the main business of the Navy was resolving triangles involving officers' wives'.[43] The social hierarchies of class and rank depicted in films such as *In Which We Serve* (1942) are less in evidence in post-war naval films such as *The Cruel Sea* (1953), where the emphasis is on leadership by ability rather than by class. The war films of the 1950s have often been read as an asser-tion of a more meritocratic social order in which leadership resides with the middle classes.[44] This also helps to explain the disappearance of the 'sons of empire' in post-war cinema as the Second World War hero (Spitfire pilot, Desert Rat, Chindit, Dam Buster) assumed pre-eminence. The old-fashioned imperial hero enjoyed a last glorious fling in *North West Frontier* (1959), though this rousing *Boy's Own* adventure yarn was tempered by the knowledge of Indian independence (1947) and the film inevitably suggests a certain equivocation about the British imperial pres-ence in India.

The emergence of more egalitarian social politics after the Second World War – itself largely a consequence of the ideology of the 'people's war' projected in wartime British film from *circa* 1942 – is demonstrated by Roy Boulting's remake of *Forever England*. In fact, *Sailor of the King* (1953) is significant for a number of reasons. It was made for a Hollywood studio (Twentieth Century-Fox) and starred an American actor (Jeffrey Hunter) in a narrative that is updated to the Second World War. Its dedication to 'the Spirit of Her Majesty's Royal Navy' is conventional enough, but what is unusual about the film is its conclusion. The film has two endings that (uniquely in my knowledge) are both included in the film, with the audience being asked to decide which they prefer and 'record your impression in cards available in the lobby'. The first ending has Andrew Brown's mother (Wendy Hiller) arriving at Buckingham Palace to receive a posthumous Victoria Cross for her son and meeting her former lover (and the boy's father) Admiral Saville (Michael Rennie). The second ending reveals that Brown survived: he collects his medal in person and is assigned as a signalman to Saville's ship. In contrast to *Forever England*, however, Saville does not learn in either version that Brown is his son. While the inclusion of both endings in the finished film would seem to suggest some confusion within the studio over its commercial prospects (the industry's rule of thumb being that a happy ending is worth more at the box office), it has the effect of overcoming the rigid social barriers presented in *Forever England*.

Sailor of the King (also known as *Single-Handed*) was one of three film adaptations of C. S. Forester in the early 1950s that were all backed by American capital: the others were *Captain Horatio Hornblower RN* (1951) and *The African Queen* (1952) produced for Warner Bros. and independent Sam Spiegel respectively. The semi-American parentage of the films is significant in explaining their narrative strategies 'that portrayed the struggle for a more egalitarian sexual and social order'.[45] Hornblower (Gregory Peck), for example, has risen through the ranks: he stands outside and to some extent aloof from a social order that he both covets and challenges. *The African Queen* similarly focuses on two outsiders – a grizzled riverboat captain (Humphrey Bogart) and a prim spinster missionary (Katherine Hepburn) – who overcome their differences to attack and sink a German gunboat on Lake Tanganyika in 1915. It is as much a character study as an adventure film, though its charismatic leads ensured its popular success.

It was during the 1950s that the war film emerged as a dominant genre of the British cinema: around 75 feature films about the Second World War were produced between 1950 and 1959.[46] These films fall into several distinct groups or lineages, including the naval epic (*The Cruel Sea*, *The Battle of the River Plate*, *Above Us the Waves*, *Sink the Bismarck!*), the war biopic (*Odette*, *The Silent Enemy*, *I Was Monty's Double*, *Reach for the Sky*, *Carve Her Name With Pride*), the prisoner-of-war drama (*The Wooden Horse*, *Albert RN*, *The Colditz Story*, *Danger Within*) and the reconstruction of particular events using real or archetypal characters (*Angels One Five*, *The Malta Story*, *The Dam Busters*, *Ice Cold in Alex*, *Dunkirk*). The critical view of these films was summed up by William Whitebait of the *New Statesman* who felt that they retreated into a comfortable nostalgia rather than facing up to present-day problems:

I think that war films, nearly all of which hark back, emotionally as well as factually, contribute more than any other source to this daydream; because if the horror of war strikes the eye more than in any other way, so does its glossing-over lull fears and angers, and creates an imaginary present in which we can go on enjoying our finest hours.[47]

Yet the critical response disguises the fact that war films were popular with cinema goers. *Odette* and *The Wooden Horse* were both in the top-ten attractions of 1950, while *The Cruel Sea* was the top film in 1953, followed by *The Dam Busters* (1955), *Reach for the Sky* (1956) and *Sink the Bismarck!* (1960). The popularity of war films suggests that, far from tiring of the war, audiences could not get enough of it.

While there are exceptions, such as *The Cruel Sea*, which examines the psychological stress endured by men at war, what is perhaps most remarkable about 1950s war films is that, by and large, they continue to represent war as an adventure. Leslie Mallory, film critic of the *News Chronicle*, complained that the British studios preferred 'the war film that makes war romantic' and pointed out that while audiences were lapping up 'Wing-Commander Kenneth More soaring through the blue with merry quip and jest', no one had yet dared to make a film of Richard Hillary's posthumously published autobiography *The Last Enemy* (1942), 'because relays of hatchet-men have been unable to prett-ify the truth and terror of real air war out of it'.[48] There is much substance to the charge that these films represent a sanitized image of war, certainly in comparison to wartime films such as *Nine Men* or *Went the Day Well?* There is little evidence in these films of the industrialized warfare that brought about the horrors of Dresden, Auschwitz and Hiroshima. The enemy is humanized once again, exemplified by the presence of sympathetic German characters (*The Battle of the River Plate*, *Ice Cold in Alex*). The focus of narrative attention has switched from wartime films, imbued as they were with the socially egalitarian ideology of the 'people's war', to heroic individuals who are usually middle-class 'good chaps' who give the impression that they regard war as a game. In *Reach for the Sky*, for example, Bader is desperate for 'one last fling before it's all over', while in *They Who Dare* an officer instructs his men to 'scrag the Jerries'.

The theme of war as a game was most apparent in the cycle of prisoner-of-war films, where escaping is presented as a sport played mostly by public-school-educated officers. The conventions of these films are remarkably consistent: Germans are humourless 'goons' who inform their captives that escape from the camp is impossible, only to be proved wrong by British ingenuity and pluck. The ethos of these films is summed up in a review of *The Colditz Story*: 'The whole thing is really an exciting game, it seems, escape being a jolly adventure in which some are more lucky than others.'[49] Critics sometimes complain that these POW films are unrealistic because they give the impression that life in camp was nothing but a series of schoolboy pranks: the favourite pastime when not escaping is making fun of the Germans, or 'goon-baiting'. Andy Medhurst, for example, dismisses them as 'pure adventure stories' and complains that 'all

The Great Escape (John Sturges, 1963).

sense of threat is dissipated by reassuring British humour, and the tone of the film (a Billy Bunter story where Mr Quelch is a Nazi) is established'.[50] It is an unfair criticism, not least because most of the films are factually based and, according to the POW memoirs on which they are based, life in camp does seem to have followed rituals not unlike boarding school. There are also differences between films in the cycle: *The Wooden Horse*, for example, suggests the tension and irritability that arises between men confined in close proximity, while *Danger Within* features an informer within the camp. *The One That Got Away* (1957) was an attempt to vary the genre in that the narrative was reversed: the film dramatizes the escape of Fritz von Werra (Hardy Kruger) from a British camp in Canada.

The summation of the POW cycle was *The Great Escape* (1963), directed by John Sturges for the US Mirish Corporation. Its American parentage is evident in the importation of Hollywood stars (Steve McQueen, James Garner) alongside the familiar

British stalwarts (Richard Attenborough, James Donald) and the film reflects their greater cultural capital: it is the more resourceful and independent Americans who survive while most of the British contingent are killed. *The Great Escape* tends to be regarded as an extreme fictionalization of the POW genre and it is true that, once outside the wire, the film includes several extremely unlikely episodes: McQueen's character Hilts, for example, steals a German motorcycle and leads his pursuers on a merry chase until he is finally recaptured, having nearly made it across the border to Switzerland. The actual details of the escape itself, however, are closely based on Paul Brickhill's book (Brickhill had himself been an inmate in Stalag Luft III at the time of the mass break-out in March 1944) and Attenborough's character Squadron-Leader Roger Bartlett is physically modelled on the real 'Big x', Roger Bushell. Oddly enough, the *Monthly Film Bulletin* felt that the details of the planning of the escape 'tend to be tedious' and that 'the most successful scenes are largely fictional'. It also averred that the film resorted to the conventional genre archetype 'with Stalag Luft North as a sort of convalescent home housing a collection of cheerful, well-fed young men whose high spirits lead them to dig tunnels'.[51] For all its heroics and jaunty music, however, *The Great Escape* is one of the few POW films to remind us of the human costs of war: fifty of the escapees are summarily shot by the SS.

    The Great Escape represents the zenith of the cinema's representation of the pleasure culture of war, and its enduring appeal is testimony to its special status in popular film culture.[52] By the 1960s, however, the nature of the war adventure film was changing. This was partly a consequence of changes in the film industry: the steady erosion of the cinema-going audience and the rise of television as a rival medium of popular entertainment. *The Great Escape* was one of a cycle of 'all-star' war epics in the early 1960s – including *The Guns of Navarone*, *Lawrence of Arabia* and *The Longest Day* – that marked the genre's transition from sober realism to all-out spectacle. This was part of the film industry's attempt to lure audiences away from their television sets and back into cinemas. The popular success of these films disguised the fact, however, that not only was the cinema-going audience in decline but its demographic composition was changing. The traditional family audience had disappeared by the 1960s (with occasional high-profile exceptions such as *The Sound of Music*) and the hard core of regular cinema-goers now comprised a younger, largely male demographic. This process was only belatedly recognized by the film industry, which for much of the 1960s clung to traditional genres and archetypes. War films in the 1960s became highly derivative: *Submarine X-1* (1967), for example, is a heavily fictionalized remake of the factually based *Above Us the Waves*, while *633 Squadron* (1964) and *Mosquito Squadron* (1968) are nothing if not virtual colour remakes of *The Dam Busters*. A consequence of the changes in the film industry – and in particular the decline in the British market – is that these nominally 'British' films had to cast American stars (James Caan, Cliff Robertson, David McCallum – the latter a British actor whose reputation had been made on American television) for the international market. It became apparent during the 1960s that the tastes of cinema audiences had shifted towards action and

Where Eagles Dare (Brian Hutton, 1968).

spectacle, preferably with liberal doses of violence and cynicism. This was reflected in the enormous popular success of the James Bond films and in the 'spaghetti westerns' of Sergio Leone, which turned Clint Eastwood into a box-office superstar. And this trend also manifested itself in the war film, through the emergence of the action-adventure as the dominant type of film. The pleasure culture of war found its most enduring and popular form in the rise of what might be called the 'special mission' film that held sway at the box office throughout the 1960s.

men on a mission

Where Eagles Dare (1969) is the apotheosis of the special-mission narrative. A mixed group of six British MI6 agents and one US Ranger are sent to rescue an American general, chief planner for the Second Front, from the impenetrable Schlöss Adler in the Bavarian Alps. They are dropped by parachute but one of the team is killed – the result not of an accident or enemy action but foul play. The commanding officer, Major Smith, meets Mary, another agent whose presence on the mission is not known to the others, and then leads the group into the village where he contacts Heidi, another agent posing as a barmaid ('You seem to have a lot of women stashed around this country, Major'). Another member of the group is murdered and three others are captured, but Smith and his second-in-command, Lieutenant Schafer, nevertheless successfully effect entry into the castle. It transpires that the American general is really an actor and that the mission is actually an elaborate deception to expose the extent of German penetration of British Intelligence. Smith extracts from the traitors the names and addresses of the entire German spy network in Britain; Schafer shoots all the German officers who have been witness to the deception. They escape from the castle via cable car and autobus, fighting a running battle with the hordes of pursuing German troops. They make it to their pre-arranged rendezvous at a nearby military airfield, where they are picked up by the RAF. On the plane Smith reveals that the chief German agent in Britain is none other than Colonel Turner, who sent them on the mission in the first place. Turner chooses to jump from the plane rather than face the hangman's noose.

Even in an industry where, as William Goldman puts it, 'nobody knows anything', *Where Eagles Dare* was nothing if not a pre-determined box-office success: two major stars (Richard Burton as Smith, Clint Eastwood as Schafer), a screenplay adapted from his own novel by Alistair MacLean (author of the highly successful *The Guns of Navarone*) and the sort of elaborate and protracted action set pieces that characterized the James Bond

Where Eagles Dare.

movies. It duly became one of the leading box-office attractions of 1969 and has remained a popular favourite ever since.[53] Most critics regarded it as undemanding hokum that was not meant to be taken seriously. The *Monthly Film Bulletin* thought it 'a magnificently ludicrous blockbuster . . . Alistair MacLean has obviously enjoyed spoofing his own work, and his cunningly devious script piles extravagance on extravagance with a sublime contempt for logic.'[54] A dissenting note was sounded by Margaret Hinxman in the *Sunday Telegraph*, however, who averred that what started out as a 'jolly good schoolboy wheeze' turned into 'a brutal, mindless bloodbath'.[55]

Robert Murphy remarks that *Where Eagles Dare* 'has little to do with the realities of the Second World War'.[56] That may be so, but it rather misses the point that the film makes no pretence to historical reality. It is unashamedly an adventure film in the best *Boy's Own* tradition and, if it is divorced from any sense of historical context, it nevertheless contributes power-fully to the celebration of the Second World War in British popular culture. *Where Eagles Dare* represents the closest approximation that the cinema has achieved to the style and ethos of British boys' comics such as *Victor*, *Commando*, *Warlord* and *Battle*. From the early 1960s war stories, often featuring commandos and other elite military units on special assignments, were a staple of British comics. As Paris observes: 'The action strip offered its readers exciting visual entertainment with a minimum of explanation or character development, and rushed the reader from one action-packed image to another.'[57] The narrative and visual style of *Where Eagles Dare* replicates the comic strip: it eschews talk in favour of bursts of explosive action and the *mise-en-scène* is fragmentary and highly stylized. A significant change from the novel, however, is that the garrulous, wise-cracking Schafer has been turned into a taciturn assassin to fit the star persona of Clint Eastwood, who kills clinically with silenced pistol or commando dagger. There are scores of deaths in *Where Eagles Dare* (I counted a possible 83) but, excepting Hinxman, the film did not provoke censure for its violence. Like the comic strip the violence is clean and bloodless: the only suggestion of a 'dirty' kill is when Shafer is shown wiping his knife afterwards.

As well as the absence of psychological realism, furthermore, *Where Eagles Dare* is also characterized by the absence of ideology. The critic Penelope Mortimer remarked that it was 'a stirring tale with not a moral in sight'.[58] Unlike most other war adventure films, it has no moments where characters question the morality of their actions or make lofty statements about the conduct of war. This is partly a consequence of its reduction of narrative causality to an almost abstract level. On one level the plot is extremely complex: an elaborate game of bluff and double bluff that at one point has Major Smith of MI6 revealed as Major Schmidt of German Intelligence, only to reveal that he has in fact been Major Smith all along ('Major, right now you've got me about as confused as I ever want to be', Shafer remarks). The best comparison here is to espionage films such as *The Spy Who Came in from the Cold* (1965) with their convoluted tales of deception, duplicity and deceit set against the moral *chiaroscuro* of the Cold War. Yet at the same time it is absurdly simple: the only function of the plot is to get its protagonists into a situation from which they have to fight their way out. To this extent the sheer implausibility of *Where Eagles Dare* works to its advantage: the film is so far detached from reality that such objections never really arise.

That *Where Eagles Dare* could be seen as a spoof or parody of genre conventions (in fact it is neither: the film plays it entirely straight) indicates that the special-mission narrative was already well established in popular cinema. Indeed, the previous twenty-five years had witnessed a large number of special-mission films in British and American cinema. Some were based on fact (*Cockleshell Heroes*, *Ill Met By Moonlight*, *The Heroes of Telemark*) while others were entirely fictitious (*They Who Dare*, *Sea of Sand*, *The Battle of the V1*, *The Guns of Navarone*, *Operation Crossbow*). The special-mission narrative emerged towards the end of the Second World War when it represented a new departure for the combat movie by importing some aspects of the resistance or spy melodrama. Thus we might see the origins of the MacLean epics in wartime British espionage films such as *Night Train to Munich*, *Secret Mission* and *The Adventures of Tartu*. There is also a continuity between wartime resistance films and post-war treatments of the work of the Special Operations Executive (SOE), including *Now It Can Be Told*, *Against the Wind*, *Odette* and *Carve Her Name With Pride*.[59] The SOE film, and American equivalents such as Fritz Lang's *Cloak and Dagger*, is a hybrid of the war and spy genres that merges the conventions of both: it focuses on clandestine operations but tends not to feature full-scale combat. The typical 'men on a mission' film, however, usually includes combat sequences and its protagonists are generally regular (or irregular) troops rather than secret agents. The SOE films tend to include more prominent roles for women than the male-centred special-mission narrative. These films represent not merely a *Boy's Own* cinema but also a 'boys only' cinema: for the most part women are conspicuously absent and even when they are not their presence is marginal.

The prototype of the special-mission narrative is Raoul Walsh's *Objective: Burma!* (1945), a late example of the Second World War combat cycle. The film sets up an objective – the

Objective: Burma! (Raoul Walsh, 1945).

destruction of a Japanese radar post deep in the Burmese jungle – and follows the men who are sent to achieve it. *Objective: Burma!* is notorious as the film that caused a minor diplomatic row when it was released in Britain: the press reacted strongly against it on the grounds that it made no reference to the role of the British Fourteenth Army in the Burma campaign and gave the impression that Errol Flynn and a platoon of Yanks won the war in the Far East single-handed. The outcry was so strong that the film had to be withdrawn by its distributor, Warner Bros., and was not shown in Britain until the 1950s.[60] This hysterical reaction has tended to diminish the reputation of what turns out to be a mature combat film notable for its unassuming heroics and its realistic representation of the physical hardships of jungle warfare. Basinger contends that it is characterized, like *They Were Expendable* and *A Walk in the Sun*, by 'a grim sense of war as a no-win situation, in which we will hang on and endure, but not without suffering'.[61] The mission is achieved but at heavy cost: half the men are killed either by the enemy or by disease in the harsh environment. The British response to the film seems all the more absurd given that it was in fact based (loosely) on real American operations in Burma by units led by Brigadier-General Frank Merrill and, unlike some later special-mission films (including British examples), does not suggest that this one operation is vital to the outcome of the war. Its reception may have been influenced by the existence of an earlier melodramatic film *Dive Bomber* (1942) – though in fact the two films are unrelated – which ends with Flynn declaring: 'Now for Burma and a crack at those Japs!'

Objective: Burma! exemplifies the psychological realism that critics have identified in the mature combat film. This was an outcome of the time at which it was made: in 1945 it would have been almost impossible to treat the war in any other way. The trajectory of the special-mission film over the next two decades can be seen in terms of a gradual shift away from psychological realism towards the pure adventure story that would reach its final form in *Where Eagles Dare*. This process was uneven and should not be seen as a linear progression. Quite often individual films exhibit a tension between the two extremes of moral seriousness about war on the one hand and the spirit of high adventure on the other. This tension is apparent in *They Who Dare* (1953), directed for British Lion by the veteran Lewis Milestone. As we might expect from the director of *All Quiet on the Western Front* and *A Walk in the Sun*, *They Who Dare* (the title refers to the famous motto of the Special Air Service 'Who Dares Wins', though the SAS is not mentioned by name in the film) is a sober, restrained

They Who Dare
(Lewis Milestone,
1954).

narrative that offers serious reflections on the nature and conduct of war. A raiding party of British commandos and Greek partisans is sent to destroy two German airfields on the island of Crete: the mission is successful, but all but two of the twelve are either killed or captured. The two survivors are Lieutenant Graham (Dirk Bogarde) and Sergeant Corcoran (Denholm Elliott) and it is through the contrast between these characters that the film debates the effective conduct of war. Graham is characterized as a reckless 'amateur' who regards war as a sport ('If we pull this one off there'll be a lot more to follow'; 'I did it for the kick'), whereas Corcoran is a moody grammar-school intellectual given to quoting Robert Burns and who openly questions Graham's leadership. This seems appropriate given that Graham nearly leads his men into a minefield and that it is Graham's insistence on planting 'one last bomb' that brings about their discovery. At the end of the film Corcoran's seething anger towards Graham comes to the surface: 'I hate you! I hate you for never giving up! You don't think. You haven't even the imagination to know when you're licked!'

Penelope Houston felt that *They Who Dare* 'is a disappointment both as an adventure story and as a study of a small group of men under strain' and complained in particular that Bogarde and Elliott 'play these parts without much conviction, and the latter's hysterical outburst on the beach strikes a singularly false note'.[62] This response, however, would seem to be conditioned by a decade of understated heroics and emotional restraint in the British war film: *They Who Dare* was perhaps the first postwar film to examine the tension behind the quiet stoicism that critics and audiences expected of British heroes. As Corcoran remarks at one moment of tension: 'How's your stiff upper lip now? Mine's hanging out like a chimpanzee's!' The film is particularly interesting for its representation of masculinity in that neither Bogarde nor Elliott really measures up to the heroic warrior ideal: Bogarde is too effete, Elliott too hysterical. It is significant in this regard that Bogarde's character is referred to throughout by his nickname of 'Boy'; this may simply be a reference to his boyish looks, but as a slang term for a homosexual man it may also be a discrete reference to the actor's sexuality. A quarter of a century later Bogarde would play the similarly blinkered, ineffectual Lieutenant-General 'Boy' Browning in *A Bridge Too Far*.

For all its dramatic flaws, however, *They Who Dare* defined many of the conventions of the special-mission narrative. Its opening, for example, establishes the historical context of the mission, through a combination of archive footage and voice-over narration explaining that the German airfields on Crete are a threat to the Eighth Army before its offensive at El Alamein. This has the effect of establishing the importance of the mission as well as reassuring audiences: no matter what the outcome of the mission, post-war audiences would know that the Eighth Army was victorious at El Alamein. The Greek islands were a favourite location for British special-mission films (*Ill Met By Moonlight*, *The Guns of Navarone*) and the tension within the commando unit would become a recurring theme.

The Guns of Navarone (1961), albeit produced on a more ambitious scale, returns to similar ground as *They Who Dare* both geographically and thematically. A mixed commando unit is sent to a Greek island to destroy two massive German guns that control the straits and are preventing the evacuation of British soldiers from another island nearby. *The Guns of Navarone* was directed by J. Lee Thompson, whose previous films included *Ice Cold in Alex* and *North West Frontier*, and produced by Carl Fore-

The Guns of Navarone (J. Lee Thompson, 1961).

man, one of the American screenwriters blacklisted by the House UnAmerican Activities Committee (HUAC). Foreman had co-written (with fellow blacklistee Michael Wilson) *The Bridge on the River Kwai* (credited on the film itself to Pierre Boulle, author of the original novel, who ironically was presented with an Academy Award for a script he had nothing to do with), and there is evidence that he intended *The Guns of Navarone* as an anti-war film in a similar vein. In the preface to a souvenir brochure for the film he wrote: 'The effort required for the production of this film will be more than justified if, in addition to providing entertainment on its own level, it will cause people to wonder when such nobility of purpose, such dedicated courage, will cease to be wasted on the senselessness of war.'[63] If the finished film can hardly be described as anti-war, it does nevertheless have aspirations to be more than just a tale of derring-do.

The Guns of Navarone punctuates its long, though tense, narrative with several scenes in which protagonists question the ethical conduct of war. Captain Mallory (Gregory Peck) is a no-nonsense pragmatist who believes that 'The only way to win a war is to be as nasty as the enemy' and who cynically lies to the wounded Major Franklin (Anthony Quayle) in the hope that Franklin, whom he calculates will be administered scopolamine by the Germans, will pass the false information on believing it to be true. Mallory's decision to leave Franklin behind brings him into conflict with Corporal Miller (David Niven). The theme of doing whatever is necessary 'to get the job done', by fair means or foul, recalls the wartime classic *The Life and Death of Colonel Blimp*, which, amongst other things, was a study of the British attitude towards war. Another moral dilemma arises in *The Guns of Navarone* when it turns out that one of the Greek partisans help-ing them, a young woman called Anna (Gia Scala), has betrayed them to the Germans: on this occasion Miller goads Mallory by referring back to his 'three choices' regarding Franklin. The question of whether cold-blooded killing is morally justifiable links *The Guns of Navarone* to a pair of late 1950s films, *Orders to Kill* and *Circle of Deception*, though here it is an incident grafted onto an adventure story rather than the main focus of the narrative. The film evokes some sympathy for Anna, who, it explains, was faced with the choice of either helping the Germans or being tortured and sent to a field brothel. The scene may be read as a metaphor for Foreman's experiences before HUAC: testify or else. In the event it is fellow partisan Maria (Irene Papas) who shoots Anna. It is inter-esting to note how often in these films it is a woman who pulls the trigger – others include *Against the Wind* (Simone Signoret) and *Operation Crossbow* (Lilli Palmer) – which perhaps suggests some-thing about the blurring of gender differences in total war.

The Guns of Navarone was a commercial and critical success, though most reviewers focused on its spectacle and narrative excitement rather than its ethical undertones.[64] An exception to this was Penelope Houston: 'The moral arguments cut into the action without extending it: there is too much diffusion, too much talk, too many themes raised and dropped so that the adventure story is not lifted to another plane but over-stretched, robbed of the tight narrative concentration needed for a mounting tension.'[65] Yet *The Guns of Navarone* seems to me to exemplify what might be called the 'intelligent epic' that was emerging in the early 1960s and was also represented by the likes of *Spartacus*, *Lawrence of Arabia* and *Zulu*, all films that successfully infused their spectacle with an ethical discourse about the nature of war. This element of the film is absent from MacLean's original novel and may reasonably be attributed to Foreman (who wrote the screenplay) rather than Thompson (who was a late replacement for Alexander Mackendrick). The film also introduces a greater complexity to the characterization, explicitly mapping out homosocial relationships within the male group. Thus *The Guns of Navarone* may be interpreted as a narrative of coupling: Gregory Peck/Anthony Quinn are one couple, David Niven/Anthony Quayle are another, Quayle is injured, Quinn leaves Peck for Irene Papas, and Peck and Niven catch each other on the rebound.

If *The Guns of Navarone* did not become the anti-war film that Foreman had intended, *The Victors* (1963), which he wrote and directed, most certainly did. Murphy categorizes *The Victors* as an anti-epic and considers that 'Foreman recreates the world of soldiers on a long-term campaign with unequalled authenticity'.[66] Contemporary critics were less sympathetic, however: Bosley Crowther complained that 'it is specious, sentimental and false to the norm of soldier nature and the realities of war'.[67] *The Victors* is an episodic narrative focusing on an American platoon from the campaign in Sicily in 1943 through Normandy to the end of the war. In many respects it seems nothing less than a highly schematic response to *The Guns of Navarone*: it concerns ordinary troops rather than members of a special unit; it is set against the background of actual campaigns rather than a fictitious special mission; and is shot in austere black and white rather than sumptuous colour. The critical and commercial failure of *The Victors* may have been due to its dour and downbeat content in a period when it was still unusual to represent the Second World War as anything other than the 'good war', though it stands up now as a bold film that was perhaps ahead of its time. Its ironic distancing from the narrative it tells – established through the inclusion of triumphalist propaganda newsreels that are contrasted with the grim reality of life in the combat zone – anticipates Kubrick's *Full Metal Jacket* by a quarter of a century.

It was the success of *The Guns of Navarone*, however, that pointed the direction for the war adventure film for the rest of the 1960s. Its influence can be seen in two similar films of 1965 – *The Heroes of Telemark* and *Operation Crossbow* – which both aspired to epic status. *The Heroes of Telemark* is the better of the two, a fictionalized account of a real raid on a German heavy-water plant in Norway that, like *The Guns of Navarone*, is posited on the dramatic tension between its central protagonists, scientist Rolf

The Dirty Dozen (Robert Aldrich, 1967).

Pedersen (Kirk Douglas) and resistance fighter Knut Straud (Richard Harris). The issue of whether to kill an informer is rehearsed again: the man is spared, only to lead German ski troops to the partisans' camp. David Robinson appreciated the film's direction: 'It is a measure of Mann's narrative ability that he very largely succeeds in controlling this dramatically diffuse material, giving it a degree of cohesion and maintaining tension through a series of action climaxes.'[68] That *Operation Crossbow* is overall rather less satisfying is due in part to its multiple narrative (it follows several agents acting independently rather than focusing on them as a group) and in part to its downbeat conclusion in which the protagonists succeed in their mission but die. Again the film rehearses a classic moral dilemma: what to do with a civilian (the divorced wife of a man whose identity has been assumed by one of the agents) who has stumbled by accident onto the plan. The *Monthly Film Bulletin*, however, felt that this device had become a genre cliché: 'Even attempts at ruthless realism – the summary shooting of Sophia Loren, for instance – turn out as just another melodramatic convention.'[69]

The moral dilemmas rehearsed in *The Guns of Navarone*, *The Heroes of Telemark* and *Operation Crossbow* exemplify the persistence of psychological realism in the adventure film during the 1960s. The films do not question that the war is just and necessary, but rather suggest that its successful prosecution involves a level of moral compromise: the end justifies the means. Towards the end of the decade, however, a greater level of cynicism was evident in the genre as it started to question the underlying assumptions of the war as a heroic enterprise. It is tempting to read films such as *The Dirty Dozen*, *The Devil's Brigade*, *Play Dirty* and *Too Late the Hero* as a response to the Vietnam War, though the first and most influential of them, Robert Aldrich's *The Dirty Dozen* (1967), was released a full two years before the My Lai massacre became public knowledge. The premise of the film is that a group of American servicemen facing execution or long terms in prison for a range of crimes, including murder and rape, are offered pardons if they volunteer for a suicide mission. The 'dirty dozen' are recruited and trained by the hard-bitten Major Reisman (Lee Marvin) who transforms them from a group of ill-adjusted misfits into an effective commando unit. The actual mission – to assassinate a group of high-ranking German staff officers on the night before D-Day – is a coda to the film (it is not even witnessed in the novel on which the film was based, where we learn what happened through an incomplete army report). The mission is successful, though all but one of the dozen are killed in action.

The Dirty Dozen was hardly an original idea – Roger Corman's *The Secret Invasion* (1964) had told a similar story on a much lower budget – but it was a huge popular success, with domestic rentals of $19.5 million. It disturbed liberal critics, however, by its apparent endorsement of war crimes. In the climactic action Reisman orders his men to pour petrol through the air vents of an underground bunker where the wives and aides of the German staff officers are sheltering and then to throw in hand grenades. It is an entirely gratuitous act: the prisoners have been confined and represent no threat to the success of the mission. Stephen Farber read this sequence as an allegory of the Holocaust, in which the audience was manipulated into identifying with the perpetrators:

> The inevitable reference would be to the gas chambers, but the film-makers don't seem to be aware of it; at any rate, they're urging us to cheer the American killers. Aldrich cuts back and forth, in standard thriller fashion, from the Germans getting closer and closer to freedom – breaking through the inner door of their deathtrap, storming the outer, untouchable doors – to the American soldies [*sic*] preparing for the explosion with greater and greater frenzy . . . Aldrich has worked the scene so skillfully that a part of us is eager, for a few seconds anyway, to see them killed.[70]

Farber concluded that 'the war being fought in the movie, though it is called World War II, is really the Vietnam War'. Even in 1967 there were some who questioned the war in Vietnam, believing that US servicemen were being indoctrinated to hate an enemy that did not pose the same threat as the Nazis.

The success of *The Dirty Dozen* prompted a cycle of cynical and noisy action films at the end of the decade in which the protagonists were as much criminals as they were soldiers. The first of these was also the least: *The Devil's Brigade* (1968) cast William Holden as the officer who whips a group of thugs and deviants into a crack fighting unit. *Play Dirty* (1969) was a British-made desert variation in which a mob of ex-criminals are sent to destroy an oil depot behind German lines. The film ends with its two main protagonists (Michael Caine, Nigel Davenport) shot whilst helping themselves to banknotes from a safe blown up during the action. The film draws an irresistible parallel between war and criminality: 'War is a criminal enterprise and I fight it with criminals', remarks the colonel who runs this irregular unit. *Play Dirty* draws parallels between the conduct of the desert war and the tactics of the ancient Egyptians, though this seems to have been too intellectual for American critics, who wrote it off as 'an anemic British relation' of *The Dirty Dozen*.[71] Aldrich returned to the genre with *Too Late the Hero* (1970), in which a reluctant US Navy officer (Cliff Robertson) joins a British raiding party to destroy a Japanese radio station on a Pacific island. The film depicts its nominal heroes as lazy ne'er-do-wells who openly discuss whether the mission would be aborted if the American (a linguist who speaks fluent Japanese) were to be killed. One of the British soldiers thinks nothing of looting his dead comrades and cutting off the finger of a dead Japanese officer to steal his ring. Roger Greenspun of the *New York Times* felt that

Kelly's Heroes (Brian Hutton, 1970).

'the action is . . . so thoroughly undercut as to render it meaning-less not only to war but also as art'.[72] The more likeable *Kelly's Heroes* (1970), director Brian G. Hutton's follow-up to *Where Eagles Dare*, crosses the war film with the crime caper movie: Clint Eastwood leads a platoon of misfits to rob gold bullion from a bank behind enemy lines. *Kelly's Heroes* reflects the counter-cultural values of the 1960s in its anachronistic hippy dialogue ('Quit making with the negative waves') and improbably mini-skirted prostitutes. Clear evidence that it is not intended to be taken seri-ously is the parody of the spaghetti western where Eastwood and his lieutenants Telly Savalas and Donald Sutherland (the good, the bald and the loony) face off against the Tiger tank that is guarding the bank.

Like other late 1960s and early 1970s genre films, *Kelly's Heroes* is something of a hybrid – an 'attempt to cross *The Dirty Dozen* with *Where Eagles Dare*'.[73] It also combines elements of comedy (the performances of Sutherland and Carroll O'Connor as an idiot general who follows in Kelly's wake dispensing medals from a box) with tragedy (the death of two of Kelly's men in a minefield). The tension between comedy and tragedy is evident elsewhere in films that attempt to satirize the conventions of the adventure film. Richard Lester's *How I Won the War* (1967) can be seen as a spoof of the special-mission narrative: the incompetent Lieutenant Goodbody (Michael Crawford) leads his platoon to play a game of cricket behind enemy lines in North Africa in order to impress an American general. Murphy contends that it 'is not entirely clear whether this is meant to be endearingly silly or bitingly satirical, and the film only reaches its proper plane of inspired anarchy when the wily shirker played by Jack MacGowan impersonates a general and punches everyone who contradicts him on the nose'.[74] A similar uncertainty pervades Michael Winner's *Hannibal Brooks* (1969), a hybrid of the adventure film and the POW film, in which Brooks (Oliver Reed), assigned to a work detail at a Bavarian zoo, develops a touching affection for an Indian elephant called Lucy and determines to take her safely to Switzerland when the zoo is bombed. Again the film mixes comedy (Brooks and his elephant continuously hinder the efforts of a group of partisans led by another escaped POW) and tragedy (the death of sympathetic 'good' German Willie). The fairy-tale caption at the end ('And they all lived happily after') sits rather uneasily with the fate of its heroine, Anna, who becomes the mistress of an SS officer ('It was either him willingly or the rest of them') who rewards her for her favours by shooting her. Consequently, *Hannibal Brooks* 'suffers from a state of chronic uncertainty about just what sort of film it is trying to be'.[75]

There is a sense in which the war adventure film had reached a state of inertia by the 1970s. On the one hand the genre was repeating itself: *Raid on Rommel* (1971) was a remake of *Tobruk* (1966), itself a remake of *Sea of Sand* (1958); *Operation Daybreak* (1975) was a curiously dated return to the wartime formula of films like *The Adventures of Tartu*; and *Murphy's War* (1971) was a virtual reworking of *The African Queen* with a merchant seaman (Peter Finch) and a missionary (Sian Phillips) sinking a German U-boat in Venezuela. *Shout at the Devil* (1976), about two soldiers of fortune (Lee Marvin and Roger Moore) in German East Africa during the First World War, is an extremely reactionary film that overlays its sink–the–battleship narrative (again influenced by *The African Queen*) with an ideological agenda that seems to have been inherited from the 'beastly Hun' propaganda of 1914: the Germans rape Marvin's daughter and murder her baby, while the chief antagonist, Fleischer, bears more than a passing resemblance to Erich von Stroheim. On the other hand, attempts to revive the spirit of the *Boy's Own* adventure yarn seemed dated and anachronistic in the wake of the new breed of violent action films. *Zeppelin* (1970) was a handsomely mounted period adventure recalling the spirit of John Buchan, but failed to make much impression at the box office. *Force Ten From Navarone* (1979) was a belated sequel to *Guns of Navarone* in which Robert Shaw and Edward Fox took the Peck and Niven parts: it lacks any real dramatic tension and the mission this time (to destroy a bridge in Yugoslavia) seems mundane in comparison to the first film with its overtones of Greek mythology. The last fling of the *Boy's Own* adventure – though in this case *Dad's Army*

The Eagle has Landed (John Sturges, 1976).

adventure would perhaps be more appropriate – was Euan Lloyd's production of *The Sea Wolves* (1980), in which a band of ageing irregulars (Gregory Peck, Roger Moore, David Niven and a supporting cast of stalwart British character actors) blow up a German radio ship in Goa harbour in 1943. Like *The Heroes of Telemark* it was based on a true story, though it bore little relation to the historical facts. Tim Pulleine thought the film resembled nothing more than 'a reunion of character actors who saw active service in the British cinema of the Fifties'.[76] Its use of Adinsell's 'Warsaw Concerto' (originally composed for the 1941 film *Dangerous Moonlight*) is a nostalgic throwback to the war itself.

Perhaps the most successful variation on the genre, in so far as it reworks old tropes but finds a new twist on them, was *The Eagle Has Landed* (1976). John Sturges's film, based on a best-selling novel by Jack Higgins, features an audacious German plot to kidnap Winston Churchill. The twist is that the protagonists are Germans and they are characterized sympathetically as dutiful soldiers who are simply doing their duty rather than as rabid Nazis. Their leader, Colonel Steiner (Michael Caine), is a veteran of the Eastern Front: his credentials as a 'good' German are established early in the film when he tries to prevent the deportation of a Jewish woman to a concentration camp. *The Eagle Has Landed* borrows from *Went the Day Well?* the motif of German parachutists taking over a sleepy English village: they are discovered when one of them jumps into the pond to save a child from drowning and his real uniform is exposed. Although, like the similarly themed *The Day of the Jackal*, the audience knows that Steiner will not achieve his objective, *The Eagle Has Landed* nevertheless generates real dramatic tension: its coda is brilliant *coup de théâtre*.

    The Eagle Has Landed is significant for several reasons, not least for its suggestion that the rehabilitation of the former enemy was now complete and that an adventure narrative of the war from the German perspective could be packaged for international markets. In this context it paved the way for other German-centred Second World War films including Sam Peckinpah's *Cross of Iron* (1977) and Wolfgang Petersen's *Das Boot* (1981). We have already seen how the latter was received in Britain not as an anti-war film but as an adventure narrative told from the German point of view. *The Eagle Has Landed* also marked the last significant box-office success for the cycle of special-mission films. The genre had persisted longer than most, but like all cycles of popular cinema it eventually ran out of residual cultural energy.

the persistence of war

Since the 1970s the war film has been less visible in the generic profile of popular cinema and clearly demarcated production trends are more difficult to map. During this period war films tended to be either romantic melodramas (*Yanks*, *Hanover Street*) or autobiographical accounts of childhood (*Empire of the Sun*, *Hope and Glory*). The persistence of traditional forms was exemplified by David Puttnam's production of *Memphis Belle* (1990), though this dramatization of the last mission of the famous B-17 was curiously less exciting than Wyler's wartime documentary of the same name. One of the most unusual war films of these years was John Huston's *Escape to Victory* (1981), in which war was reduced literally to a game: a football match between a team of Allied prisoners and a German team staged for propaganda, which culminates in the mass escape of the Allied team. The film is chiefly notable for its casting of an array of non-acting real international footballers (including Bobby Moore, Pelé, Osvaldo Ardiles and Werner Roth) alongside non-footballing film stars (Michael Caine as ex-West Ham and England captain John Colby and a bizarrely cast Sylvester Stallone as the most unlikely goalkeeper in soccer history). John Ramsden has argued that *Escape to Victory* actually subverts the conventions of the POW film ('Your escaping is just some bloody upper crust game', the working-class officer Colby tells the escape committee), though the main cultural project seems to be to reinforce the association between England/Germany football contests and the Second World War exemplified in jokes such as: 'We've beaten them twice at their national game, it's about time we beat them once at ours.'77

There are a number of possible explanations for the decline of the war film during the 1980s and '90s. With the Second World War now too distant an event to form part of the memory of the teenagers and young adults who comprised the bulk of the cinema audience, the myths and archetypes of the conventional war film ceased to hold any cultural relevance, while more recent wars such as Vietnam did not lend themselves to heroic treatment except by proxy (*Rambo*). The war film had been displaced in popular cinema by the rise of science fiction and fantasy films (*Star Wars*, *Star Trek*) and by contemporary action adventure films (*Commando*, *Lethal Weapon*, *Die Hard*). It is usually a sign that a genre has run its course, furthermore, when it becomes the subject of parody and spoof. It might be argued that films such as *Top Gun* and *Rambo* were largely self-parodies anyway on account of their extreme narcissism: *Hot Shots!* (disturbed pilot joins an elite task force to raid an accordion factory) and *Hot Shots!: Part Deux* (special forces sent to the Middle East to rescue another special forces team) were lamentably unfunny spoofs that make the originals seem like masterpieces in comparison. *Down Periscope*, similarly, was a spoof of submarine films (*Run Silent, Run Deep*, *Up Periscope!*, *The Hunt for Red October*, *Crimson Tide*) that assumed its audience would be familiar with the conventions of the genre and delight in sending them up.

What happened to the pleasure culture of war during these years? It might be thought that the relative decline of the war film in popular cinema would have signalled an end to the

The Dam Busters
(Michael Ander-
son, 1954)

Star Wars (George
Lucas, 1977)

phenomenon. While the war film itself has been less visible in
recent decades, however, the pleasure culture associated with it is
manifest in other genres, especially science fiction and fantasy.
Indeed, there is an argument to make that these films can be
understood as disguised combat films in so far as they borrow
conventions and motifs from the genre. *Star Wars* (1977) is a

Lining up with a
bouncing bomb.

Delivering the proton
torpedoes.

crucial film in this respect. *Star Wars* is usually seen as a pastiche
of the space opera adventure serials of the 1930s (*Flash Gordon*,
Buck Rogers), though in fact it deploys a wide range of filmic
references including sword-and-sorcery adventures, westerns
(especially *The Searchers*) and even *The Wizard of Oz* (Chewbacca
the Wookie as the uncowardly lion). One of its points of reference
is the aerial combat film, specifically *The Dam Busters*. Indeed, the
climax of *Star Wars* makes so many narrative and visual references to *The Dam Busters* that it is unfeasible to see it as anything
other than a highly schematic pastiche. The pilots (Rebel
Alliance/617 Squadron) attack an imposing enemy target (Death
Star/the Ruhr dams) with a special weapon (proton torpe-

does/bouncing bomb) in the face of heavy anti-aircraft fire (turbo-lasers/flak), while scenes of the attack are inter-cut with scenes in the control room where the backroom crew wait anxiously for news. It is no coincidence that Gilbert Taylor, the director of photography for *Star Wars*, was responsible for special effects photography on *The Dam Busters*. George Lucas's script also uses dialogue that appears to have been lifted wholesale from the earlier film:

> *Gibson:* How many guns do you think there are, Trevor?
> *Trevor Roper:* I'd say they're about ten guns – some in the field and some in the towers.

> *Gold Leader:* How many guns do you think, Gold Five?
> *Gold Five:* I'd say about thirty guns – some on the surface, some in the towers.

And:

> *Gibson:* I'll fly across the dam as you make your run and try to draw the flak off you.

> *Gold Leader:* I'm going to cut across the axis and try and draw their fire.

And again as the first bombs/torpedoes strike the target:

> *Dave:* It's gone! We've done it!
> *Gibson:* We haven't. It's still there.

The Dam Busters.

Star Wars.

> *Gold Five:* It's a hit!
> *Gold Leader:* Negative, negative. It didn't go in. Just impacted on the surface.

The similarities here are simply too close to be coincidental: to this extent *Star Wars* can be seen as a disguised war film. Indeed, the *Star Wars* films have been interpreted as an allegory of the Second World War (the Galactic Empire's minions are cloned 'stormtroopers'), simply transposing the narrative of resistance to Fascism to 'a galaxy far, far away'.

If this reading seems somewhat fanciful, then the association between science fiction and the war film is more explicit in what has been called 'military SF'. Films such as *Aliens* (1986), *Stargate* (1994), *Independence Day* (1996) and *Starship Troopers* (1997) transpose the conventions of the combat movie to outer space, merely substituting 'bugs' for 'Jerries' or 'Japs'. There is a sense in which these films displace political and racial 'otherness' onto their extra-terrestrial invaders: their makers can hardly be blamed for perpetuating negative stereotypes of bug-eyed monsters. *Independence Day* is nothing if not an uncredited remake of H. G. Wells's *The War of the Worlds*, except that on this occasion the invaders are destroyed not by the intervention of nature but through a combination of American scientific ingenuity and military power: the climax even features the US president, a former fighter pilot, climbing back into the cockpit 'to kick some alien butt'. *Starship Troopers*, based on a militaristic Cold War novel by SF author Robert A. Heinlein, posits a futuristic war between the human race and giant arachnids. The film provoked censure for its 'almost non-stop use of fascist imagery'.[78] It would be more appropriate to see the film, directed by Paul Verhoeven, as a satire: it refers ironically to Second World War propaganda through a recruiting broadcast called *Why We Fight* (also the title of Frank Capra's documentary series made to explain the war to US servicemen), in which patriotic citizens declare 'I'm doing my part' and 'The only good bug is a dead bug.' Yet the film also bears a close relationship to the conventions of the combat film. Andrew O'Hehir suggests that '*Starship Troopers* clearly follows the pattern of numerous war pictures: a group of civilians is moulded into a warrior band and tested in the crucible of combat where some are killed and others hardened'.[79] The television series *Space: Above and Beyond* (1995–6) belongs to the same military SF genre: the theme of the series was 'about the nature of war . . . what it was like to be at war'.[80]

Films like *Independence Day* and *Starship Troopers* represent a jingoistic, gung-ho attitude towards war that can also be seen in novels, comics and video games. When I began writing this book the Second World War-themed *Code of Honour* was being advertised as 'the first great shoot-'em-up of 2006'. The pleasure culture of war is evidently alive and well in the gaming sphere. Such games have recently attracted censure from moral campaigners for their violence – thus taking their place in a lineage of moral panics that also includes film, comic books and 'video nasties' – though their effects on their consumers remain difficult to ascertain. Even the producers of these games are unclear on this issue, as Martin Knight, the chairman of DID Interactive Computer Games, remarked in reference to his game *Wargasm*:

> Some people may argue it condones war. I really don't know, the jury is out. I don't have an opinion on whether our products in particular have that effect. But historically there was no such thing as computer games or similar entertainments and we've fought wars for ever.[81]

The rise of interactive computer and video games based on the combat experience is itself partly a consequence of the revival of the combat movie in recent years. The success of *Saving Private Ryan* revived interest in a genre that many thought had become moribund: Spielberg's film was followed within a few years by *The Thin Red Line*, *Enemy at the Gates*, *Pearl Harbor*, *U-571*, *Windtalkers*, *Saints and Soldiers*, *Flags of Our Fathers* and the television series *Band of Brothers*. The Vietnam combat film has reappeared after an absence of a decade (*We Were Soldiers*) and there have been films about the Gulf War (*Three Kings*) and Somalia (*Black Hawk Down*). While these films are very different in subject matter, the critical mass over the last decade is testimony to the impact and influence of *Saving Private Ryan*. It is also, partly, a consequence of advances in computer-generated graphics – advances that were themselves an outcome of the gaming industry – that permit increasingly 'realistic' representations of combat. To the list above may be added others that are not war films as such but are nevertheless associated with the cycle due to their battle sequences, such as the American Civil War drama *Cold Mountain* or the historical epic *Gladiator*. The role of CGI in representing war as spectacle, meanwhile, is showcased by the battle sequences of ancient world epics such as *Troy* and mythical adventures such as *The Lord of the Rings*.

What is more, however, is the extent to which recent combat movies simultaneously represent war as a terrible experience whilst also valorizing the heroism of those who take part in it. There has been a shift away from the 'war is hell' theme of the combat films of the 1980s (including Second World War films such as Samuel Fuller's *The Big Red One*, as well as Vietnam films such as *Platoon* and *Full Metal Jacket*) and towards the idea that while war is unpleasant it is also necessary and justifiable. While these films still represent the chaos of war, there is an underlying sense of fighting for a cause. The theme of these films is 'fighting the good fight' and their protagonists are characterized as honourable and patriotic.[82] Even Vietnam can now be reclaimed in this context, as *We Were Soldiers* demonstrates. The films also promote an idealized image of the comradeship of the military. Their recurring theme is the idea of brotherhood (described literally in the title of *Band of Brothers*) and they focus on the special bond that exists between servicemen. Far from despising war, these films present it as a heroic enterprise that only those who have experienced it can properly understand.

The revival of the combat film can be related to political and ideological factors as well as to advances in film technology. The collapse of the Soviet Union in the early 1990s left the United States as the world's only superpower and brought into sharp focus the issue of American foreign policy. To this extent films like *Saving Private Ryan* and *Pearl Harbor* have been seen in the context of a narrative of American global leadership that presents American military power as a benign and necessary influence on world events. The shots of the Stars and Stripes that bookend *Saving Private Ryan*, for example, 'underline the pivotal role played by the US in securing freedom not just for Ryan and other Americans but also for the world'.[83] This projection of American military power becomes all the more significant in the context of a rising level of popular anti-Americanism in certain parts of the world, most particularly throughout the Middle East, which was thrown into even sharper relief by the al Qaeda-sponsored terrorist attacks on New York and Washington on 11 September 2001. The pro-interventionist narratives of *Black Hawk Down* and *We Were Soldiers* – both films that were in production before 9/11 but that were hurried to completion – take on an even greater ideological significance in the context of the 'War on Terror'. These films suggest that intervention in trouble spots such as Somalia and Vietnam is justified: there is no room for questioning US foreign policy. One commentator described *Black Hawk Down*, for example, as 'an astonishing glorification of slaughter that makes the tragedy look like a majestic triumph for the brotherhood of man, rather than a humbling defeat for the United States'.[84] A partial exception to this is *Three Kings* (1999), which questions the motives for US involvement in the Gulf War as a captured American is tortured by his Iraqi captor to confess that the war was fought for the control of oil. *Three Kings* is essentially a reversioning of *Kelly's Heroes*, in which a motley crew embark on a private mission to 'liberate' Kuwaiti gold from the Iraqis. Its extreme stylization – a description of how septicaemia sets in following a bullet wound is illustrated by a computer graphic of the body's internal organs in what seems like a spoof medical documentary – led to it being described as an 'MTV war film'. This impression was reinforced by the presence of rapper Ice Cube as one of the three protagonists alongside former boy band member Mark Wahlberg and legitimate screen star George Clooney. On this occasion the resolution is ultimately moralistic: the mercenaries give back the gold in return for the release of rebels being held by the Iraqi Republican Guard. Yet, as John Wrathall remarked in *Sight and Sound*:

> What lingers in the mind far longer than the smart dialogue, the slightly cartoon characterisations or the neat feel-good ending is a vivid sense of the sickening nature of modern warfare: poison-gas, land-mines,

cluster bombs, chemical pollution, torture chambers and the indiscriminate slaughter of civilians.[85]

Other films of the Gulf War have lent themselves to more conventional treatments, such as *Courage Under Fire* (1996), in which a dead US servicewoman (played by America's then sweetheart Meg Ryan) is posthumously awarded the Congressional Medal of Honor. In Britain, meanwhile, the 'men on a mission' narrative was revived in two television versions of first-hand accounts of the war by former members of the Special Air Service. In contrast to the films of the 1950s and '60s, however, they were both accounts of a mission that failed. *The One That Got Away* (1996) – perhaps an ironic reference to the POW film of the same title – starred Paul McGann as Chris Ryan, the member of an SAS patrol who evaded capture by making an arduous and lonely trek to safety in Syria, while *Bravo Two Zero* (1998) starred Sean Bean as the leader of the same patrol, Andy Macnab. *The One That Got Away* was the more critical of the two stories, implying that the mission failed because it was too hurriedly conceived and not properly equipped, though both are essentially glowing endorsements of the courage, toughness and fighting skills of the SAS. *Bravo Two Zero* features an extended firefight in which the eight-man patrol holds off a vastly numerically superior force, while *The One That Got Away* includes an authentic incident during which Ryan single-handedly destroys two Iraqi vehicles that locate him in the desert. These television films can be placed in a lineage of narratives celebrating Britain's elite military regiment that also includes the film *Who Dares Wins* (1981), produced by Euan Lloyd (*The Wild Geese*, *The Sea Wolves*) in the wake of the successful resolution of the Iranian Embassy siege in London in May 1980.[86]

The popularity of the SAS biopics suggests that the pleasure culture of war remains as much an aspect of popular culture as it has always been. The persistence of this tradition was further demonstrated in 2003 by the success of Peter Weir's film *Master and Commander: The Far Side of the World*, which provides a fitting conclusion to this chapter since it illustrates the political and cultural economies of the film industry in the early twenty-first century. On the one hand this rousing sea-faring adventure, adapted from the novels of the Anglo-Irish writer Patrick O'Brian, is a glorious throwback to the traditional virtues of the historical adventure yarn. *Screen International*, for example, called it a 'good-natured, old-fashioned romp that combines attention to detail, well-acted characterisation, and a fast-paced pursuit story'.[87] And the Internet magazine *Box Office Online* thought it 'an old-fashioned seafaring spectacle of the Errol Flynn–Douglas Fairbanks variety . . . [that] hearkens back to an era when such films were able to be thoughtful, even artistic'.[88] On the other hand the film is a combination of British cultural capital (the literary source material and most of the supporting cast) with Hollywood dollars (the \$135 million budget was put up by Twentieth Century-Fox, Universal and Miramax). It also revised the source material in line with the ideological and cultural imperatives of the contemporary film industry. Thus, while O'Brian's novel on which it was largely based, *The Far Side of the World*, had been set during the Anglo–American War of

Master and Commander: The Far Side of the World (Peter Weir, 2003).

1812 and featured a British frigate, HMS *Surprise*, in pursuit of an American raider, USS *Norfolk*, the film version switches the events to 1805 and the enemy vessel becomes a French privateer, the *Acheron*. Released as it was six months after the invasion of Iraq, an action that was opposed by France, *Master and Commander* was seized upon by some commentators as an example of the popular Francophobia that swept the United States and Britain in 2003. As A. O. Scott remarked in the *New York Times*, 'It is tempting to read some contemporary geopolitical relevance into this film, which appears at a moment when some of the major English-speaking nations are joined in a military alliance against foes we sometimes need to be reminded do not actually include France.'[89] Perhaps a more reasonable explanation, however, is that the domestic box office would be unlikely to tolerate a film in which the Americans were represented as the villains of the piece. It is symptomatic of Hollywood's commercial strategies that it should rewrite history for its own convenience: *U-571* (2000) had provoked controversy in Britain not unlike the reception of *Objective: Burma!* when it depicted the US Navy rather than the British capturing the Enigma decoding machine.

Master and Commander is an example of the intelligent epic that, like *Lawrence of Arabia* and *Zulu*, combines its massive action set pieces with a literate script and rounded character-izations and performances. The central dynamic is the friend-ship between Captain Jack Aubrey (Russell Crowe) and ship's surgeon Stephen Maturin (Paul Bettany). Aubrey and Maturin represent different archetypes of masculinity: one the bluff man-of-action whose courage and inspirational leadership locate him squarely in the tradition of Hornblower and Nelson, the other the quiet, erudite man-of-science whose ability as a surgeon (at one point in the film Maturin has to operate on himself to remove a bullet after being accidentally shot) earns the respect of the crew. The narrative ideologies of *Master and Commander* are indeed old-fashioned, invoking the motif of the ship as a microcosm of the nation familiar from such films as *In Which We Serve*. Aubrey and his crewmen are bound by an ethic of duty ('subject to the requirements of the service') that unites all members of the crew regardless of class or rank. HMS *Surprise*, like Coward's HMS *Torrin*, represents the national community. This is made explicit when Aubrey makes a patriotic declaration to stir his men before the climactic battle: 'England is under threat of invasion and though we be on the far side of the world, this ship is our home. This ship is England.' This invocation of patriotism – done entirely straight and without irony – locates *Master and Commander* squarely within a popular representation of war that harks back, culturally and ideologically, to the cinema of the 1930s and '40s.[90]

A prominent feature of cultural history in recent years has been its recognition of the extent to which popular cinema contributes to discourses of nationhood and national identity. On the one hand, we no longer accept the old-fashioned idea that national identity is an entirely naturalized phenomenon that is somehow inherent in the air we breathe and the land we walk upon, nor, on the other hand, do we readily accept the view of the intellectual left that national identity is an entirely false or artificial ideology that is promoted by ruling elites to encourage social cohesion and support for the nation state. The trend in recent scholarship, following Benedict Anderson's notion of 'imagined communities', is to regard most forms of identity as being constructed: constructed by history, by politics, by geography, by religion, by institutions and by culture. Films such as *Master and Commander* exemplify the processes through which popular culture influences, even determines, our understanding of history and nationhood. Its critical and popular success (it grossed some $215 million worldwide) would seem to suggest that the version of history represented by the film accorded with popular tastes. To this extent we can reasonably conclude that the old-fashioned ideologies of duty, service and patriotism, far from being redundant at the beginning of the twenty-first century, remain as important for cinema audiences as they have ever been. And the film exemplifies the persistence of a tradition of representing war as a heroic and rightful enterprise as well as an arena for displaying the qualities of courage, leadership and masculinity that have always been central to the promotion of the pleasure culture of war. Far from deploring war, films such as *Master and Commander* positively thrive upon it. It is a tradition that, arguably, has been more enduring than the various cycles of anti-war cinema that have come and gone at different periods. And it suggests that popular cinema still has a role to play in conditioning publics to accept war as a legitimate means for the resolution of international disputes, as well as providing potent fantasies of heroism and adventure. The *Boy's Own* legacy, it would seem, is alive and well in the early twenty-first century.

conclusion

This book has offered a necessarily selective and inevitably much condensed overview of the different modes through which the subject of war has been represented in popular cinema. I have cast my net as widely as possible and have drawn on examples from the films of the United States, Britain, France, Italy, Germany, Poland and the Soviet Union. Given such a vast field it is difficult to draw any hard-and-fast conclusions about the representation of war: the picture is one of a wide range of narratives and styles. Films about war have ranged from gung-ho heroics to out-and-out pacifism and the image of war itself from grim reality to cartoonish adventure. The fact that different modes of representing war have often coexisted in popular cinema (barely a year separates *Rambo* and *Platoon*, for example) would suggest that no single mode predominates. Rather, the range of images and representations suggests a complex and often ambiguous response to war by both film-makers and their audiences.

Yet it is possible to make a few general remarks about the relationship between war and film. The most significant, perhaps, is that this relationship is a two-way process: while war has shaped film, film has also shaped war. Film came of age as a medium during the century of total war and it is instructive to note how many major film-makers have turned to the subject at one point or another: D. W. Griffith, G. W. Pabst, Jean Renoir, John Ford, Michael Powell, Andrzej Wajda, Andrei Tarkovskii, Sergei Bondarchuk, Akira Kurosawa, David Lean, Stanley Kubrick and Steven Spielberg are amongst those who have made films about war. Other significant directors who have made forays into the genre at one point or another include King Vidor, Raoul Walsh, René Clement, John Huston, Anthony Mann, J. Lee Thompson, Samuel Fuller, Robert Aldrich, Joseph Losey, Tony Richardson, Richard Attenborough, Sam Peckinpah, Louis Malle, Francis Ford Coppola, Wolfgang Petersen, Peter Weir, Oliver Stone and Ridley Scott. Lewis Milestone's reputation rests entirely on two of the war films he directed (*All Quiet on the Western Front*, *A Walk in the Sun*). Perhaps the principal reason why war has proved an attractive subject to film-makers of such very different hues is that it provides ideal cinematic material, combining human drama and tragedy on the one hand with the spectacle of conflict on the other. And drama and spectacle have always been the basic elements of popular film.

Furthermore, war has determined the economic and aesthetic histories of film. It was as a consequence of the disruption wrought upon European film production during the First World War, for example, that the US film industry was able to establish the position of global hegemony that it enjoys to this day. The Second World War created the conditions for the 'wartime wedding' of documentary and the fiction film in Hollywood as well as in Britain, and that a few years later enabled the emergence of Italian Neo-realism as a distinctive style and movement. East European film industries came of age after the Second

World War and drew much of their initial cultural energy from their complex response to that conflict. It might even be argued that the apocalyptic fantasy offered by films such as the *Lord of the Rings* trilogy is in some way related to the so-called War on Terror, representing as it does a Manichean conflict between the forces of light and darkness.

At the same time, however, film has determined popular impressions of what war is like. From *The Battle of the Somme* to the reporting of the Gulf, Bosnia and Iraq wars, film has purported to show the reality of war even while it has resorted to artifice in doing so. It is still not unusual for extracts from *All Quiet on the Western Front* to feature in television programmes about the First World War because they are more dramatic than the 'real' thing. The popular response to films such as *Saving Private Ryan*, acclaimed for their realism and authenticity, suggests that the public at large have become conditioned to accepting the filmic representation of war as being like the real thing. From here it is only a short step to the idea of 'virtual war' and the notion that we experience war through its representation rather than through the actuality.

There is much evidence, moreover, to indicate the extent to which the images of war represented in film have influenced society at large. On its most mundane level this can be seen in the way in which several British war films of the 1950s, including *The Colditz Story*, *The Dam Busters* and *Ice Cold in Alex*, became reference points for television commercials in the 1990s, often for lager. More significantly, it is clear that the ideals of heroism, masculinity and comradeship represented in film have influenced those who have fought in war. Films such as *Sands of Iwo Jima* and *To Hell and Back* (the film biography of America's most decorated Second World War hero, Audie Murphy) have been cited by Vietnam veterans as influencing their decision to enlist. *Top Gun* is held responsible for an increase in recruitment to the US Air Force and there is little doubt that the books and subsequent television films of *Bravo Two Zero* and *The One That Got Away* did much to enhance the reputation of Britain's Special Forces and to stimulate public awareness of their role in the Gulf War.

As a genre the war film is dominated, unsurprisingly, by films about the two World Wars. While the image of the First World War is consistent across different national cinemas, the narrative of the Second World War tends to be told predominantly from a national perspective since each nation tells its own stories through its films. This is inevitable in biopics of national heroes and heroines (*Reach for the Sky*, *The Star of Africa*, *Lucie Aubrac*), but it is also evident in the representation of crucial events that conform to particular national narratives (*Kanal*, *Stalingrad*, *The Winter War*). It is perhaps only to be expected that each nation will use its cinema to tell war stories that endorse a peculiarly national perspective: Russian films focus on 'the Great Patriotic War', British films on 'their finest hour' and French films on the narrative of national resistance. These war narratives are also influenced by the conditions of the present: the allegorical strategies of Wajda, for example, or the critical engagement with the legacy of the Occupation in films such as *Lacombe, Lucien*.

An issue that runs throughout the filmic representation of war is the tension between showing the 'true' nature of combat and revelling in the spectacle of it. This tension has been a recurring feature since the contemporary reception of *The Battle of the Somme* revealed the grim fascination with images of death on the battlefield. Even when films attempt to expose the brutality and ugliness of war they still invite us to watch it: to this extent *Come and See* is as much a film of spectacle as *Saving Private Ryan*. The visual pleasures of war are perhaps best experienced at a safe distance from reality, whether in the comic-strip violence of *Where Eagles Dare* and *Rambo* or in the historical spectacles of *Henry V* and *War and Peace*. Those two latter films belong to an era of cinema that has now passed: while the conduct of modern warfare has become increasingly mediated by technology so, too, has its visual representation in film. In the twenty-first century opposing armies can be generated through special effects without requiring the proverbial 'casts of thousands': the fantasy battlefields of *The Lord of the Rings* have become the standard against which future films will be judged.

There is more to the war film, however, than simply the reconstruction of battles and the dramatization of heroism and suffering. The war film is often a vehicle for allegory: it is sometimes as significant for what it says about the present as what it says about the past. The Second World War, in particular, has a wide range of meanings depending upon the context: reliving past glories in the face of imperial decline (Britain), exorcizing the memory of Fascism (Germany) or collaboration (France), and interpreting the resistance to Fascism in the light of present political circumstances (Poland). The most common allegorical intent of the war film is to make a statement about the futility and horror of war itself: ironically the genre is condemning the very subject that sustains its existence. This ambiguity is often a feature of the most acclaimed war films, from *All Quiet on the Western Front* to *Full Metal Jacket*.

I suggested in the Introduction that I was not making any claims for the aesthetic and cultural merits of individual films. One criterion by which the war film is often judged, to an even greater extent than other genres, is realism. On this basis a film such as *La Grande Illusion* would generally be considered superior to, say, *The Great Escape*, though both focus on the experiences of airmen who have become prisoners of war. Yet the range of film styles included in this book would suggest that realism is not the only mode of representation that has been adopted. As this book has demonstrated, the representation of war has ranged from the understated heroics of *The Dam Busters* to the flag-waving propaganda of *The Green Berets*, from the austerity of *Nine Men* to the bloated spectacle of *Apocalypse Now*, from the psychological intensity of *Paths of Glory* to the theatrical stylization of *Oh! What a Lovely War*, and from the claustrophobic realism of *Das Boot* to the panoramic desert landscapes of *Lawrence of Arabia*. This range of styles is eloquent testimony both to the different strategies that film-makers have employed for representing war and to the diverse tastes of cinema audiences. It is a truism to remark that war has been a major factor in shaping the modern world. What I hope this study has demonstrated is that war and its representation have also been significant factors in shaping the history of film.

references

introduction

1 Steve Neale, *Genre and Hollywood* (London, 2000), p. 125.

2 See, for example, a standard reference work such as *Halliwell's Film and Video Guide*, ed. John Walker (London, 1977, and subsequent editions).

3 Jeanine Basinger, *The World War II Combat Film: Anatomy of a Genre*, rev. edn (Middletown, CT, 2003), pp. 67–75.

4 John Whiteclay Chambers II, '*All Quiet on the Western Front* (1930): The Antiwar Film and the Image of the First World War', *Historical Journal of Film, Radio and Television*, XIV/4 (1994), p. 377.

5 Examples of this historiography include: Gilbert Adair, *Hollywood's Vietnam: From 'The Green Berets' to 'Full Metal Jacket'*, 2nd edn (London, 1989); Anthony Aldgate and Jeffrey Richards, *Britain Can Take It: The British Cinema in the Second World War* (Oxford, 1986); Basinger, *The World War II Combat Film*; John Whiteclay Chambers II and David Culbert, eds, *World War II, Film and History* (New York, 1996); Bernadette Kester, *Film Front Weimar: Representations of the First World War in German Films of the Weimar Period, 1919–1933* (Amsterdam, 2003); Andrew Kelly, *Cinema and the Great War* (London, 1996); Roger Manvell, *Films and the Second World War* (London, 1974); Robert Murphy, *British Cinema and the Second World War* (London, 2000); and Michael Paris, ed., *The First World War and Popular Cinema: From 1914 to the Present* (Edinburgh, 1999).

6 Paul Virilio, *War and Cinema: The Logistics of Perception*, trans. Patrick Camiller (London, 1989), p. 1.

7 Baudrillard's assertion about the Gulf War arose from an article in *Liberation* on 29 March 1991. A translated version was published as *The Gulf War Did Not Take Place* (Bloomington, IN, 1993). For a sustained critique of Baudrillard and others, see Christopher Norris, *Uncritical Theory: Postmodernism, Intellectuals and the Gulf War* (London, 1992).

8   In May 2005 Channel 4 broadcast a two-part programme entitled *The 100 Greatest War Movies*, based on a poll of viewers. While the presence of *Saving Private Ryan* at no. 1 and *Apocalypse Now* at no. 2 would surprise no one, *The Great Escape* came in at no. 3, *The Guns of Navarone* at no. 14 and *Where Eagles Dare* at no. 21. Conversely, a feature in a popular film magazine demonstrated a more orthodox preference for anti-war films, with a top five of *Apocalypse Now*, *Dr Strangelove*, *Paths of Glory*, *Das Boot* and *La Grande Illusion*. See 'The Top 40 War Films', *Film Review*, 41 (2002), pp. 19–43.

1   war as spectacle

1   'Panoramic and Personal Visions of War's Anguish', *New York Times* (24 July 1998), p. 17.

2   *Saving Private Ryan* was voted best film of the year by the *New York Times*, *USA Today* and *Time* and by critics' groups in New York, Chicago, Toronto and London. It won five Academy Awards: Best Director (Spielberg), Best Cinematography (Janusz Kaminski), Best Editing (Michael Kahn), Best Sound and Best Sound Effects Editing. The Best Picture Award went to *Shakespeare in Love* (dir. John Madden, 1998).

3   *Saving Private Ryan* took $216,119,491 at the US box office to 23 May 1999 and $224,700,000 at the non-US box office to 20 December 1998 (*www.imdb.com/title/tto120815/business*).

4   'Director Delivers x-Rating on his Real-Life War Epic', *Guardian* (18 July 1998), p. 14.

5   Phil Landon, 'Realism, Genre and *Saving Private Ryan*', *Film and History*, XXVIII/3–4 (1998), p. 58.

6   *Chicago Sun-Times* (24 July 1998), p. 19.

7   *The Times* (10 September 1998), p. 37.

8   'A Christian Epic', *Evening Standard* (24 July 1998), p. 9.

9   'On the Beach', *Sight and Sound*, new series, VIII/9 (September 1998), p. 34.

10   'An Internet Discussion of *Saving Private Ryan*', *Film and History*, XXVII/3–4 (1998), p. 77.

11   'Spielberg War Film Reawakens Veterans' Fears', *The Times* (29 July 1998), p. 10

12   'Is This How It Was?', *Daily Telegraph Weekend Magazine* (8 August 1998), p. 2.

13   Ambrose's endorsement was used in the press book for the film by the UK

distributor UIP: *Saving Private Ryan* (London, 1998), p. 15.

14 For example, *War Stories: Mark Cousins talks to Steven Spielberg* (BBC2, 13 September 1998) and *Return to Normandy* (BBC1, 7 September 1998) – television documentaries coinciding with the UK release of *Saving Private Ryan*.

15 For an illuminating comparison of *Saving Private Ryan* and actuality combat footage, see Toby Haggith, 'D-Day Filming – For Real: A Comparison of "Truth" and "Reality" in *Saving Private Ryan* and Combat Film by the British Army's Film and Photographic Unit', *Film History*, XIV/3–4 (2002), pp. 332–53.

16 'The Last Great War', *American Cinematographer*, LXXIX/8 (1998), p. 34.

17 'An Internet Discussion of *Saving Private Ryan*', p. 75.

18 Ibid., p. 76.

19 John A. Nesbit, 'Numbing Experience of SPR Redeems Baby Boomers', 25 January 2000: *www.imdb.com/title/tt0120815* [accessed November 2005].

20 Quoted in Trevor B. McCrisken and Andrew Pepper, *American History and Contemporary Hollywood Film* (Edinburgh, 2005), p. 103.

21 Robert Kolker, *A Cinema of Loneliness: Penn, Stone, Kubrick, Scorsese, Spielberg, Altman*, 3rd edn (Oxford, 2000), p. 131.

22 Haggith, 'D-Day Filming – For Real', pp. 339 and 348.

23 André Bazin, 'The Myth of Total Cinema', in *What Is Cinema?*, ed. and trans. Hugh Gray (Berkeley, CA, 1969), vol. I, p. 21.

24 Rudolf Arnheim, *Film as Art*, trans. L. M. Sieveking and Ian F. D. Morrow (London, 1958), p. 55.

25 Laurent Ditman, 'Made You Look: Towards a Critical Evaluation of Steven Spielberg's *Saving Private Ryan*', *Film and History*, XXVIII/3–4 (1998), p. 68.

26 John Ellis, *Visible Fictions: Cinema, Television, Video*, rev. edn (London, 1992), pp. 6–7.

27 Ibid., p. 7.

28 Landon, 'Realism, Genre and *Saving Private Ryan*', p. 59.

29 Ibid.

30 See, for example, Albert Auster, '*Saving Private Ryan* and American Triumphalism', *Journal of Popular Film and Television*, XXX/2 (2002), pp. 98–104.

31 Derek Malcolm, 'Saving the Director's Bacon', *Guardian* (6 August 1998), Section 2, p. 11.

32 'An Internet Discussion of *Saving Private Ryan*', p. 79.

33 Quoted in Edward Lowery, 'Edwin J. Hadley: Travelling Film Exhibitor', *Journal of the University Film Association*, XXVII/3 (1976), p. 6.

34 Quoted in Charles Musser, *The History of the American Cinema*, vol. I: *The Emergence of Cinema: The American Screen to 1907* (Berkeley, CA, 1990), p. 31.

35 Pierre Sorlin, 'War and Cinema: Interpreting the Relationship', *Historical Journal of Film, Radio and Television*, XIV/4 (1994), p. 359.

36 Quoted in Anthony Aldgate, *Cinema and History: British Newsreels and the Spanish Civil War* (London, 1979), p. 3.

37 Erik Barnouw, *Documentary: A History of the Non-Fiction Film*, rev. edn (New York, 1993), p. 24.

38 Rachael Low and Roger Manvell, *The History of the British Film, 1896–1906* (London, 1948), p. 68.

39 W.K.-L. Dickson, *The Biograph in Battle: Its Story in the South African War* (London, 1901).

40 Ibid., p. xiii.

41 Simon Popple, 'But the Khaki-Covered Camera is the *Latest* Thing: The Boer War Cinema and Visual Culture in Britain', in *Young and Innocent? The Cinema in Britain, 1896–1930*, ed. Andrew Higson (Exeter, 2002), p. 13.

42 Quoted in Peter Jelavich, 'German Culture in the Great War', in *European Culture in the Great War: The Arts, Entertainment and Propaganda, 1914–1918*, ed. Aviel Roshwald and Richard Stites (Cambridge, 1999), p. 42.

43 Sorlin, 'War and Cinema', p. 360.

44 Nicholas Reeves, *Official British Film Propaganda During the First World War* (London, 1986), p. 25.

45 Quoted in Jelavich, 'German Culture in the Great War', p. 38.

46 See Reeves, *Official British Film Propaganda During the First World War*, pp. 94–113. A more sceptical assessment of the film's value as propaganda is provided by S. D. Badsey, '*The Battle of the Somme*: British War-Propaganda', *Historical Journal of Film, Radio and Television*, III/2 (1983), pp. 99–15

47 *The Bioscope* (24 August 1916), p. 671.

48 *The Times* (1 September 1916), p. 7.

49 D. S. Higgins, ed., *The Private Diaries of Sir H. Rider Haggard, 1914–1925* (London, 1980), p. 84.

50 Roger Smither, '"A Wonderful Idea of the Fighting: The Question of Fakes in *The Battle of the Somme*', *Historical Journal of Film, Radio and Television*,

XIII/2 (1993), pp. 149–68.

51 Ibid., p. 160.

52 Nicholas Reeves, 'Cinema, Spectatorship and Propaganda: *Battle of the Somme* (1916) and Its Contemporary Audience', *Historical Journal of Film, Radio and Television*, XVII/1 (1997), p. 23.

53 Smither, '"A Wonderful Idea of the Fighting"', p. 150.

54 See G. H. Malins, *How I Filmed the War* (London, 1920), *passim*.

55 Michael Paris, 'Enduring Heroes: British Feature Films and the First World War, 1919–1997', in *The First World War and Popular Cinema: 1914 to the Present*, ed. Paris (Edinburgh, 1999), p. 56.

56 Stephen Pendo, *Aviation and the Cinema* (Metuchen, NJ, 1985), p. 74.

57 Aldgate, *Cinema and History*, p. 98.

58 John Grierson, 'The Course of Realism', in *Grierson on Documentary*, ed. Forsyth Hardy (London, 1966), p. 72.

59 Basil Wright, *The Long View: A Personal Perspective on World Cinema* (London, 1974), p. 200.

60 David Welch, *Propaganda and the German Cinema, 1933–1945* (Oxford, 1983), p. 118.

61 Haggith, 'D-Day Filming – For Real', p. 344.

62 Donald Bull, 'Filming D-Day', *Documentary News Letter*, VI/2 (1945), p. 90.

63 Quoted in Wright, *The Long View*, p. 208.

64 Quoted in Winston S. Churchill, *The Second World War*, vol. IV: *The Hinge of Fate* (London, 1951), p. 675.

65 Jeffrey Richards and Dorothy Sheridan, eds, *Mass-Observation at the Movies* (London, 1987), pp. 220–91.

66 Barnouw, *Documentary*, p. 163.

67 *The Times* (23 November 1942), p. 5.

68 James Chapman, '"The Yanks Are Shown to Such Advantage": Anglo-American Rivalry in the Production of *The True Glory* (1945)', *Historical Journal of Film, Radio and Television*, XVI/4 (1996), pp. 533–54.

69 *The Listener* (8 August 1945), p. 231.

70 Charles Barr, 'War Record', *Sight and Sound*, LIV/4 (1989), p. 265.

71 Memorandum from Jeremy Isaacs to 'All Second World War Personnel', 4 October 1972, held by the Film and Video Archive of the Imperial War Museum, London. On the making of *The World at War*, see James Chapman, '*The World at War*: Television, Documentary, History', in *Television, the Historian and Television History*, ed. Graham Roberts and Philip M.

Taylor (Luton, 2001), p. 137.

72 David Robinson, 'It Happened Here', *Sight and Sound*, XXXIV/1 (1964–5), p. 39.

73 Mike Wayne, *Political Film: The Dialectics of Cinema* (London, 2001), pp. 5–24. See also Irene Bignardi, 'The Making of *The Battle of Algiers*', *Cineaste*, XXV/2 (2000), pp. 14–22.

74 Stephen Farber, 'Shooting at Wars', *Film Quarterly*, XXI/2 (1967–8), p. 27.

75 Nancy Ellen Dowd, 'Popular Conventions', *Film Quarterly*, XXII/3 (1969), pp. 26–7.

76 *Documentary News Letter*, II/12 (December 1941), p. 221.

77 John Shearman, 'Wartime Wedding', *Documentary News Letter*, VI/54 (1946), p. 53.

78 Jeanine Basinger, *The World War II Combat Film: Anatomy of a Genre*, rev. edn (Middletown, CT, 2003), p. 136.

79 Roger Manvell, *Films and the Second World War* (London, 1974), p. 101.

80 *New York Times* (2 September 1942), p. 9.

81 *New York Times* (4 June 1943), p. 17.

82 *New York Times* (18 November 1943), p. 29.

83 *New York Times* (27 January 1945), p. 15.

84 *New York Times* (25 August 1945), p. 7.

85 *New York Times* (21 December 1945), p. 25.

86 *New York Times* (6 October 1945), p. 9.

87 *New York Times* (31 December 1949), p. 9.

88 *New York Times* (12 November 1949), p. 8.

89 *New York Times* (28 January 1950), p. 10.

90 *New York Times* (6 January 1951), p. 9.

91 *New York Times* (20 September 1956), p. 29.

92 *The Times* (14 May 1942), p. 6

93 *The Times* (27 January 1943), p. 6.

94 *The Times* (23 November 1942), p. 5.

95 *Monthly Film Bulletin*, X/110 (February 1943), p. 13.

96 Eric Rhode, *A History of the Cinema from its Origins to 1970* (London, 1976), p. 372.

97 *The Times* (24 July 1941), p. 6.

98 *The Times* (19 October 1942), p. 6.

99 *The Times* (23 June 1943), p. 6.

100 *The Times* (10 November 1944), p. 6.

101 *The Times* (20 May 1943), p. 6.

102 *The Times* (17 May 1955), p. 3.

103 Andy Medhurst, '1950s War Films', in *National Fictions: World War Two in British Films and Television*, ed. Geoff Hurd (London, 1985), p. 58.

104 André Bazin, 'Bicycle Thief', in *What Is Cinema?*, ed. and trans. Hugh Gray (Berkeley, CA, 1969) , vol. II, p. 47.

105 André Bazin, 'The Evolution of the Language of Cinema', in *What Is Cinema?*, vol. I, p. 29.

106 Richard Winnington, *Drawn and Quartered: A Selection of Weekly Film Reviews and Drawings* (London, 1948), p. 83.

107 John Ramsden, 'Refocusing "The People's War": British War Films of the 1950s', *Journal of Contemporary History*, XXXIII/1 (1998), p. 45.

108 *New York Times* (5 October 1962), p. 28.

109 *Monthly Film Bulletin*, XXVII/313 (July 1960), p. 94.

110 *Monthly Film Bulletin*, XXV/294 (July 1958), p. 84.

111 *Monthly Film Bulletin*, XXVI/307 (August 1959), p. 104.

112 *New York Times* (30 May 1961), p. 8.

113 Richard Taylor, *Film Propaganda: Soviet Russia and Nazi Germany*, 2nd edn (London, 1999), p. 100.

114 *New York Times* (27 December 1960), p. 35.

115 Quoted in Kristin Thompson and David Bordwell, *Film History: An Introduction* (New York, 1994), p. 537.

116 *New York Times* (18 December 1965), p. 76.

117 *New York Times* (11 November 1965), p. 36.

118 William Goldman, *Adventures in the Screen Trade: A Personal View of Hollywood and Screenwriting* (London, 1984), pp. 281–2.

119 *New York Times* (10 March 1966), p. 26.

120 *Monthly Film Bulletin*, XXXII/383 (December 1965), p. 179.

121 *Monthly Film Bulletin*, XXXVI/430 (November 1969), p. 179.

122 *Monthly Film Bulletin*, XLIV/522 (July 1977), p. 142.

123 Haggith, 'D-Day Filming – For Real', p. 344.

124 Quoted in Thomas Docherty, *Projections of War: Hollywood, American Culture and World War II* (New York, 1993), p. 262.

125 Letter from Sir Laurence Olivier to George H. Macy, 7 February 1951, Laurence Olivier Archive Films 3/5, held by the British Library Department of Manuscripts. On the production of *Henry V*, see James Chapman, *Past and Present: National Identity and the British Historical Film* (London,

2005), pp. 113–42.

126 John Coleman, 'Loose Rein', *New Statesman* (19 April 1968); *Monthly Film Bulletin*, XXXV/414 (July 1968), p. 98.

127 Quoted in Kevin Brownlow, *The Parade's Gone By . . .* (London, 1968), p. 56.

128 *New York Times* (19 August 1979), Section II, p. 15.

129 Joanna Bourke, *An Intimate History of Killing: Face-to-Face Killing in Twentieth Century Warfare* (London, 2000), p. 28.

130 Jeremy Black, *Rethinking Military History* (London, 2004), p. 12.

131 Michael Ignatieff, *Virtual War: Kosovo and Beyond* (London, 2000), p. 3.

132 Jean Baudrillard, 'The Gulf War Did Not Take Place', p. 306.

133 James Der Derian, *Virtuous War: Mapping the Military-Industrial-Media-Entertainment Network* (Boulder, CT, 2001), *passim*.

134 Max Hastings, *Bomber Command* (London, 1979), p. 95.

135 Dai Vaughan, *Portrait of an Invisible Man: The Working Life of Stewart McAllister, Film Editor* (London, 1983), p. 79.

136 Paul Virilio, *War and Cinema: The Logistics of Perception*, trans. Patrick Camiller (London, 1988), *passim*.

137 Philip M. Taylor, *War and the Media: Propaganda and Persuasion in the Gulf War* (Manchester, 1992), p. 252.

138 *Sight and Sound*, new series, LV/7 (July 2005), p. 42.

139 *Sight and Sound*, new series, VII/11 (November 1997), p. 56.

140 Michael Atkinson, 'Cinema as Heart Attack', *Film Comment*, XXXIV/1 (1998), p. 45.

2 war as tragedy

1 Quoted in Louis Menashe, 'Patriotic Gauze, Patriotic Gore: Russians at War', *Cineaste*, XXIX/3 (2004), p. 29.

2 Nigel Fountain, 'The Horror, the Horror', *Guardian* (26 April 1999), Section 2, p. 10.

3 The title of the film is sometimes translated as *Go and See* or *Come and Behold*; I have opted for the most familiar version. Klimov had originally intended to call the film *Killing Hitler* but turned instead to a quotation from the Book of Revelations: 'And I saw when the Lamb opened one of the seals, and I heard, as it were the noise of thunder, one of the four beasts

saying, Come and see' (Revelations 6. 1).

4   David Robinson, 'From Russia, with Hate', *The Times* (20 March 1987), p. 19.

5   Alexander Walker, 'Brutal but True', *Evening Standard* (19 March 1987), p. 33.

6   Diane Jacobs, 'War Wounds', *Village Voice* (17 February 1987), p. 72.

7   Philip French, *The Observer* (22 March 1987), p. 23.

8   Mark Le Fanu, 'Partisan', *Sight and Sound*, LVI/2 (1987), p. 140.

9   Robin Bust, 'Descent into Hell', *Times Educational Supplement* (10 April 1987), p. 26.

10 Walter Goodman, 'Unreal Realism', *New York Times* (6 February 1987), p. C–4.

11 Virginia Dignam, 'Witness to Atrocities', *Morning Star* (20 March 1987), p. 8.

12 Virginia Mather, 'On the Eastern Front', *Daily Telegraph* (20 March 1987), p. 18.

13 Rostislav Pospelov, 'Come and See', *Soviet Film*, 12 (1985), p. 14.

14 David Denby, *New York* (23 February 1987), p. 64.

15 David Robinson, *The Times* (17 July 1985), p. 8.

16 Philip Bereson, 'Grand Opening', *What's On* (19 March 1987), p. 89.

17 David Austin, 'Worlds Gone Mad', *Spectator* (4 April 1987), p. 46.

18 Quoted in publicity material for *Come and See* produced by Cannon Film Distributors Ltd, on the microfiche for the film held by the National Library of the British Film Institute.

19 Denise J. Youngblood, 'Post-Stalinist Cinema and the Myth of World War II: Tarkovskii's *Ivan's Childhood* (1962) and Klimov's *Come and See* (1985)', *Historical Journal of Film, Radio and Television*, XIV/4 (1994), p. 418.

20 Laurence Rees, *War of the Century* (London, 2000), based on the four-part BBC/History Channel television documentary of the same title.

21 John Wrathal, 'Excursion to Hell', *Sight and Sound*, new series, XIV/2 (2004), p. 29.

22 The idea of 'counter-cinema' was originally advanced by Peter Wollen in an analysis of Jean-Luc Godard's *Vent d'est* (1969). See Wollen's *Readings and Writings: Semiotic Counter-Strategies* (London, 1982), pp. 93–106.

23 Derek Malcolm, 'The Wounds of War', *Guardian* (7 November 1985), p. 13.

24 See Christopher Browning, *Ordinary Men: Reserve Police Battalion 101 and*

the Final Solution in Poland (London, 1992); Daniel J. Goldhagen, *Hitler's Willing Executioners: Ordinary Germans and the Holocaust* (New York, 1996); and N. J. Finkelstein and R. B. Birn, *A Nation on Trial: The Goldhagen Thesis and Historical Truth* (New York, 1998).

25 Michael T. Isenberg, *War on Film: The American Cinema and World War 1* (London, 1981), p. 69.

26 Quoted in Andrew Kelly, *Cinema and the Great War* (London, 1997), p. 103.

27 'A Note from Jean Renoir', preface to *La Grande Illusion*, trans. Marianne Alexandre and Andrew Sinclair (London, 1968), p. 8.

28 Quoted in Robert Hughes, ed., *Film: Book 2 – Films of Peace and War* (New York, 1962), p. 183.

29 Pierre Sorlin, 'War and Cinema: Interpreting the Relationship', *Historical Journal of Film, Radio and Television*, XIV/4 (1994), p. 362.

30 Jay Winter, *Sites of Memory, Sites of Mourning: The Great War in European Cultural History* (Cambridge, 1995), p. 1.

31 Samuel Hynes, *A War Imagined: The First World War and English Culture* (London 1990), p. 45.

32 See Kelly, *Cinema and the Great War*, passim. On *All Quiet on the Western Front* itself, see also Andrew Kelly, *Filming All Quiet on the Western Front: 'Brutal Cutting, Stupid Censors, Bigoted Politicos'* (London 1998).

33 Quoted in Alan Burton, 'Death or Glory? The Great War in British Film', in *British Historical Cinema*, ed. Claire Monk and Amy Sargeant (London, 2002), p. 31.

34 Sorlin, 'War and Cinema', p. 363.

35 Quoted in Kelly, *Filming All Quiet on the Western Front*, p. 113.

36 Bernadette Kester, *Film Front Weimar: Representations of the First World War in German Films of the Weimar Period, 1919–1933* (Amsterdam, 2003), p. 137.

37 Ibid., p. 138.

38 Kelly, *Filming All Quiet on the Western Front*, p. 162.

39 Burton, 'Death or Glory? The Great War on British Film', p. 35.

40 *Monthly Film Bulletin*, XXXVI/424 (May 1969), p. 94.

41 The controversy that the revisionist view attracted was evident, for example, in the highly critical response to the documentary *Timewatch – Haig: The Unknown Soldier* (BBC2, July 1996).

42 G. D. Sheffield, '"Oh! What a Futile War": Representations of the Western Front in Modern British Media and Popular Culture', in *War, Culture and*

the Media: Representations of the Military in 20th Century Britain, ed. Ian Stewart and Susan L. Carruthers (Trowbridge, 1996), p. 62.

43 Niall Ferguson, *The Pity of War* (London, 1998), p. xxxii.

44 See S. D. Badsey, '*Blackadder Goes Forth* and the "Two Western Fronts" Debate', in *The Historian, Television and Television History*, ed. Graham Roberts and Philip M. Taylor (Luton, 2001), pp. 113–25.

45 Julian Petley, 'Over the Top', *Sight and Sound*, LVI/2 (1987), pp. 126–31.

46 Malcolm Smith, *Britain and 1940: History, Myth and Popular Memory* (London, 2000), p. 1.

47 Quoted in Mark Pittaway, 'Dealing with Dictatorship: Socialism and the Sites of Memory in Contemporary Hungary', in *War, Culture and Memory*, ed. Clive Emsley (Milton Keynes, 2003), p. 270.

48 Quoted in Paul Coates, *The Red and the White: The Cinema of People's Poland* (London, 2005), p. 184.

49 *Monthly Film Bulletin*, XVII/194 (February–March 1950), p. 27.

50 Kristin Thompson and David Bordwell, *Film History: An Introduction* (New York, 1994), p. 475.

51 Clifford Lewis and Carroll Britch, 'Andrzej Wajda's War Trilogy: A Retrospective', *Film Criticism*, X/3 (1986), p. 27.

52 Quoted in Anthony Bukoski, 'Wajda's *Kanal* and Mrozek's *Tango*', *Literature/Film Quarterly*, XX/2 (1992), p. 133.

53 *Films and Filming*, V/11 (August 1959), p. 20.

54 Dina Iordanova, *Cinema of the Other Europe: The Industry and Artistry of East Central European Film* (London, 2003), pp. 81–2.

55 Izabela Kalinowska, 'Changing Meanings of Home and Exile: From *Ashes and Diamonds* to *Pan Tadeusz*', in *The Cinema of Andrzej Wajda: The Art of Irony and Defiance*, ed. John Orr and Elzbieta Ostrowska (London, 2003), p. 68.

56 Sabine Hake, *German National Cinema* (London, 2002), p. 123.

57 Thomas Elsaesser, 'Defining DEFA's Historical Imaginary: The Films of Konrad Wolf', in *European Cinema: Face to Face with Hollywood* (Amsterdam, 2005), p. 337. See also Anthony S. Coulson, 'Paths of Discovery: The Films of Konrad Wolf', in *DEFA: East German Cinema, 1946–1992*, ed. Seáán Allan and John Sandford (New York, 1999), pp. 164–82.

58 Edward M. V. Plater, 'Helmut Käutner's Film Adaptation of *Des Teufels General*', *Literature/Film Quarterly*, XXII/4 (1994), pp. 253–64.

59 Hake, *German National Cinema*, p. 97.

60 Pierre Sorlin, *European Cinemas, European Societies, 1939–1990* (London,

1991), pp. 76–7.

61 *Monthly Film Bulletin*, XXXXIX/580 (May 1982), p. 81.

62 *New York Times* (24 May 1995), p. 22.

63 Tytti Soila, Astrid Söderbergh Widding and Gunnar Iversen, *Nordic National Cinemas* (London, 1998), p. 93.

64 Quoted in Philip French, ed., *Malle on Malle* (London, 1993), p. 103.

65 Quoted in Alison Smith, *French Cinema in the 1970s: The Echoes of May* (Manchester, 2005), p. 173.

66 Susan Sontag, 'Fascinating Fascism', in *Movies and Methods Volume 1*, ed. Bill Nichols (Berkeley, CA, 1976), pp. 31–43; first published in *New York Review of Books* (6 February 1975), as a review of a book on Leni Riefenstahl.

67 Philip French, 'Holocaust: Hollow Laughs', *Observer Review* (14 February 1999), p. 6.

68 Francine Stock, 'Tears for a Clown', *New Statesman* (12 February 1999), p. 43.

69 Penelope Houston, 'The Fate of F3080', *Sight and Sound*, LIV/2 (1984), pp. 93–8. An edited version of the film was shown on Channel 4 in Britain in 1984 and on PBS in the United States in 1985.

70 Ora Gelley, 'Narration and the Embodiment of Power in *Schindler's List*', *Film Criticism*, XXII/2 (1997–8), pp. 22–3.

71 Michael Medved, *Hollywood vs America* (New York, 1992), p. 227.

72 Gary Wills, *John Wayne: The Politics of Celebrity* (London, 1997), p. 233.

73 Ian McKellar, 'Apocalypse, Now and Then', *National Post* (10 July 2001), p. B-6.

74 Philippa Gates, '"Fighting the Good Fight": The Real and the Moral in the Contemporary Hollywood Combat Film', *Quarterly Review of Film and Video*, XXII/4 (2005), p. 299.

75 *Monthly Film Bulletin*, LIV/639 (April 1987), p. 123.

76 Quoted in William H. Hagen, '*Apocalypse Now* (1979): Joseph Conrad and the Television War', in *Hollywood as Historian: American Film in a Cultural Context*, ed. Peter C. Rollins (Lexington, KY, 1983), p. 231.

77 Marsha Kinder, 'The Power of Adaptation in *Apocalypse Now*', *Film Quarterly*, XXXIII/2 (1979–80), pp. 12–20.

78 Thomas Doherty, 'Full Metal Genre: Stanley Kubrick's Vietnam Combat Movie', *Film Quarterly*, XLII/2 (1988–9), p. 24.

79 Rich Schweitzer, 'Born to Kill: S. Kubrick's *Full Metal Jacket* as Historical Representation of America's Experience in Vietnam', *Film and History*,

xx/3 (1990), p. 67.

80 Doherty, 'Full Metal Genre', p. 24.

3   war as adventure

1   'An Outbreak of Rambomania', *Time* (14 June 1985), p. 52.

2   *Variety* (1 June 1985), p. 23.

3   David Denby, 'Blood Simple', *Time* (3 June 1985), p. 72.

4   Vincent Canby, 'Sylvester Stallone Returns as Rambo', *New York Times* (22 May 1985), p. 23.

5   Pauline Kael, *New York* (17 June 1985), p. 117.

6   J. Hoberman, 'Seasons in Hell', *Village Voice* (28 May 1985), p. 66.

7   'Ban this Sadistic Film, Urges MP, *Western Mail* (10 August 1985), p. 3.

8   Virginia Dignam, 'No Credibility and No Sense', *Morning Star* (30 August 1985), p. 4.

9   Alexander Walker, 'The Ugliest American in History . . . ', *Standard* (22 August 1985), p. 24.

10   Francis Wheen, 'The Incredible Hulk', *New Statesman* (30 August 1985), p. 29.

11   Adam Mars-Jones, 'Last Blood?', *New Society* (6 September 1985), p. 342.

12   Quoted in Richard Maltby, *Hollywood Cinema: An Introduction* (Oxford, 1995), p. 385.

13   Quoted in Mark Taylor, *The Vietnam War in History, Literature and Film* (Edinburgh, 2003), p. 142.

14   From an archive extract of a Reagan speech, which was included alongside clips from *Rambo* on *The 100 Greatest War Movies* (Channel 4, May 2005). *Rambo* came in, incidentally, at no. 100.

15   Taylor, *The Vietnam War in History, Literature and Film*, p. 141.

16   Ibid., p.142.

17   Quoted in 'An Outbreak of Rambomania', *Time* (24 June 1985), p. 53.

18   David Bhagat, 'Rambling Rambos', *The Spectator* (10 August 1985), p. 14.

19   Richard Shickel, 'Danger: Live Moral Issues', *Time* (27 May 1985), p. 40.

20   Vincent Canby, '"Rambo" Delivers A Revenge Fantasy', *New York Times* (26 May 1985), p. 11.

21   David Robinson, 'Stirring appeal to national paranoia', *The Times* (30 August 1985), p. 9.

22   Kael, *New York* (17 June 1985), p. 117.

23 Yvonne Tasker, *Spectacular Bodies: Gender, Genre and the Action Cinema* (London, 1993), p. 7.

24 Jeffrey Richards, *Films and British National Identity: From Dickens to Dad's Army* (Manchester, 1997), p. 170.

25 Peter Ackroyd, 'The Sneering Torso', *The Spectator* (7 September 1985), p. 29.

26 Janet Maslin, 'Sylvester Stallone's Hit Formula', *New York Times* (30 May 1985), p. C–22.

27 Carol Fry and Christopher Kemp, 'Rambo Agonistes', *Film/Literature Quarterly*, XXIV/4 (1996), p. 372.

28 Harvey R. Greenberg, 'Dangerous Recuperations: *Red Dawn*, *Rambo*, and the New Dacaturism', *Journal of Popular Film and Television*, XV/2 (1987), p. 69.

29 Graham Dawson, *Soldier Heroes: British Adventure, Empire and the Imagining of Masculinities* (London, 1994), p. 4.

30 Michael Paris, *Warrior Nation: Images of War in British Popular Culture, 1850–2000* (London, 2000), p. 69.

31 Joanna Bourke, *An Intimate History of Killing: Face-to-Face Killing in Twentieth-Century Warfare* (London, 1999), p. 16.

32 Jeffrey Richards, *The Age of the Dream Palace: Cinema and Society and Britain, 1930–1939* (London, 1984), *passim*.

33 Geoff Brown, ed., *Walter Forde* (London, 1977), p. 35.

34 *Kinematograph Weekly* (23 May 1935), p. 25.

35 *World Film News*, I/12 (1937), p. 26.

36 Jeffrey Richards, '"Patriotism with Profit": British Imperial Cinema in the 1930s', in *British Cinema History*, ed. James Curran and Vincent Porter (London, 1983), pp. 245–56.

37 Rainer Rother, 'The Experience of the First World War and the German Film', in *The First World War and Popular Cinema: 1914 to the Present*, ed. Michael Paris (Edinburgh, 1999), p. 235.

38 Ibid., p. 239.

39 Quoted in Rolf Giesen, *Nazi Propaganda Films: A History and Filmography* (Jefferson, NC, 2003), p. 57.

40 Cary Nathenson, 'Fear of Flying: Education to Manhood in Nazi Film Comedies: *Glücksinder* and *Quax, der Bruchpilot*', in *Cultural History Through a National Socialist Lens: Essays on the Cinema of the Third Reich*, ed. Robert C. Reimer (Woodbridge, 2000), pp. 96–7.

41 Michael Paris, *From the Wright Brothers to Top Gun: Aviation, Nationalism*

and Popular Cinema (Manchester, 1995), pp. 94–5.

42 Jeffrey Richards, 'Wartime Cinema Audiences and the Class System: The Case of *Ships With Wings* (1941)', *Historical Journal of Film, Radio and Television*, VII/2 (1987), pp. 129–41.

43 *Documentary News Letter*, II/12 (December 1941), p. 225.

44 John Ramsden, 'Refocusing "The People's War": British War Films of the 1950s', *Journal of Contemporary History*, XXXIII/1 (1998), pp. 35–63; Neil Rattigan, 'The Last Gasp of the Middle Class: British War Films of the 1950s', in *Re-Viewing British Cinema, 1900-1992: Essays and Interviews*, ed. Wheeler Winston Dixon (Albany, NY, 1994), pp. 143–53.

45 Sue Harper and Vincent Porter, *British Cinema of the 1950s: The Decline of Deference* (Oxford, 2003), p. 269.

46 Paris, *Warrior Nation*, p. 225.

47 William Whitebait, 'Bombardment', *New Statesman* (5 April 1958), p. 432.

48 Leslie Mallory, 'Balcon Stakes His Prestige on "Dunkirk"', *News Chronicle* (13 March 1958), p. 6.

49 *Monthly Film Bulletin*, XXI/224 (May 1954), p. 65.

50 Andy Medhurst, '1950s War Films', in *National Fictions: World War Two in British Films and Television*, ed. Geoff Hurd (London, 1985), p. 35.

51 *Monthly Film Bulletin*, XXX/355 (August 1963), p. 118.

52 *The Great Escape* came third in Channel 4's poll of *The 100 Greatest War Movies* (May 2005). In 2002 the theme music of the film was used in television coverage of the World Cup and a 'Word Cup Special Edition' DVD of the film was issued.

53 *Where Eagles Dare* was placed twenty-first in the same Channel 4 poll. One of the commentators ('journalist' James Brown) averred: '"Broadsword calling Danny Boy. Broadsword calling Danny Boy" . . . You can't hear those words and not know that that film is *Where Eagles Dare*'.

54 *Monthly Film Bulletin*, XXXVI/442 (March 1969), p. 63.

55 *Sunday Telegraph* (26 January 1969).

56 Robert Murphy, *British Cinema and the Second World War* (London, 2000), p. 251.

57 Paris, *Warrior Nation*, p. 231.

58 *Observer Review* (26 January 1969).

59 Murphy, *British Cinema and the Second World War*, pp. 90–102.

60 Ian Jarvie, 'Fanning the Flames: Anti-American Reaction to *Objective Burma* (1945)', *Historical Journal of Film, Radio and Television*, I/2 (1981),

pp. 117–37.

61 Jeanine Basinger, *The World War II Combat Film: Anatomy of a Genre*, rev. edn (Middletown, CT, 2003), p. 121.

62 *Monthly Film Bulletin*, XXI/242 (March 1954), pp. 37–8

63 Quoted in Steve Chibnall, *J. Lee Thompson* (Manchester, 2000), p. 267.

64 Ibid., pp. 272–4.

65 *Monthly Film Bulletin*, XXVIII/329 (June 1961), p. 76.

66 Murphy, *British Cinema and the Second World War*, p. 253.

67 *New York Times* (20 December 1963), p. 21.

68 *Financial Times* (26 November 1965).

69 *Monthly Film Bulletin*, XXXII/378 (July 1965), p. 112.

70 Stephen Farber, 'Shooting at Wars', *Film Quarterly*, XXI/2 (Winter 1967–8), p. 39.

71 *New York Times* (20 February 1969), p. 54.

72 *New York Times* (21 May 1970), p. 46.

73 *Monthly Film Bulletin*, XXXVII/442 (November 1970), p. 227.

74 Murphy, *British Cinema and the Second World War*, p. 248.

75 *Monthly Film Bulletin*, XXXVI/424 (May 1969), p. 102.

76 *Monthly Film Bulletin*, XXXXVII/559 (August 1980), p. 160.

77 John Ramsden, 'England versus Germany, Soccer and War Memory: John Huston's *Escape to Victory* (1981)', *Historical Journal of Film, Radio and Television*, XXVI/4 (2006), pp. 579–80.

78 'Starship Stormtroopers', *Sight and Sound*, new series, VIII/1 (January 1998), p. 5.

79 *Sight and Sound*, new series, VIII/1 (January 1998), p. 54.

80 Jan Johnson-Smith, *American Science Fiction TV: Star Trek, StarGate and Beyond* (London, 2004), p. 137.

81 Quoted in Paris, *Warrior Nation*, p. 259.

82 Philippa Gates, '"Fighting the Good Fight": The Real and the Moral in the Contemporary Hollywood Combat Film', *Quarterly Review of Film and Video*, XXII/4 (2005), pp. 297–310.

83 Trevor B. McCrisken and Andrew Pepper, *American History and Contemporary Hollywood Film* (Edinburgh, 2005), pp. 120–21.

84 Sue Williams, 'Films That Trade on Violence', *World Press Review*, IL/4 (April 2002), p. 41.

85 *Sight and Sound*, new series, X/3 (March 2000), p.5 5.

86 See Mark Connelly and David R. Willcox, 'Are You Tough Enough: The

Image of the Special Forces in British Popular Culture, 1939–2004', *Historical Journal of Film, Radio and Television*, XXV/1 (2005), pp. 1–25.

87 *Screen International* (14 November 2003), p. 28.

88 *Box Office Online Reviews*, no date: *www.boxoffice.com/scripts* [accessed May 2006].

89 *New York Times* (14 November 2003):
    movies2.nytimes.com/mem/movies/review.html [accessed May 2006].

90 James Chapman, '"This Ship Is England!": History, Politics and National Identity in *Master and Commander: The Far Side of the World* (2003)', in *The New Film History: Sources, Methods, Approaches*, ed. James Chapman, Mark Glancy and Sue Harper (London, 2007), pp. 55–68.

select filmography

The subject area is so vast that any attempt at providing a comprehensive filmography would be futile in the extreme. What follows, therefore, is a highly selective and, it must be said, extremely idiosyncratic list of those films I have viewed (or in many cases re-viewed) during the period when I was preparing this book. Most of the American and British sound films are available on retail DVD. International Historic Films (www.IHFfilm.com) is the best supplier of French, German, Polish and Russian films.

Adventures of Werner Holt, The (*Die Abenteuer des Werner Holt*) (GDR, DEFA, dir. Joachim Kunert, 1965)

All Quiet on the Western Front (USA, Universal, dir. Lewis Milestone, 1930)

Apocalypse Now (USA, United Artists/Zoetrope, dir. Francis Ford Coppola, 1979)

Ashes and Diamonds (*Popiól i Diament*) (Poland, Film Polski, dir. Andrzej Wajda, 1958)

Attack! (USA, United Artists/Independent Producers, dir. Robert Aldrich, 1956)

Au revoir, les enfants (France, Nouvelle Editions de Films, dir. Louis Malle, 1987)

Ballad of a Soldier (USSR, Mosfilm, dir. Grigori Chukrai, 1958)

Battle of Algiers, The (Algeria/Italy, Casbah Films, dir. Gillo Pontecorvo, 1965)

Battle of Britain (GB, Paramount, dir. Guy Hamilton, 1969)

Battle of the Rails (*La bataille du rail*) (France, CGFC, dir. René Clément, 1946)

Battle of the Somme, The (GB, Topical Committee for Films, dir. Geoffrey Malins and J. B. McDowell, 1916)

Big Parade, The (USA, M-G-M, dir. King Vidor, 1925)

Big Red One, The (USA, United Artists/Lorimar, dir. Samuel Fuller, 1980)

Birth of a Nation, The (USA, Epoch, dir. D. W. Griffith, 1915)

Black Hawk Down (USA, Columbia/Jerry Bruckheimer, dir. Ridley Scott, 2002)

Blighty (GB, Gainsborough/Piccadilly, dir. Adrian Brunel, 1926)

Boat, The (*Das Boot*) (GFR, Columbia/Bavaria, dir. Wolfgang Petersen, 1981)

Border Street (Poland, Film Polski, dir. Aleksander Ford, 1949)

Bridge on the River Kwai, The (GB, Columbia/Sam Spiegel, dir. David Lean, 1957)

Bridge Too Far, A (GB, United Artists/Joseph E. Levine, dir. Richard Attenborough, 1977)

Brotherhood (*Taegukgi*) (South Korea, Showbox/Kangjegyu, dir. Kang Je-Gyu, 2004)

Burma Victory (GB, Army Film and Photographic Unit, dir. Roy Boulting, 1945)

Casualties of War (USA, Columbia, dir. Brian De Palma, 1989)

Charge of the Light Brigade, The (USA, Warner Bros., dir. Michael Curtiz, 1936)

Charge of the Light Brigade, The (GB, United Artists/Woodfall, dir. Tony Richardson, 1968)

Come and See (*Idi i smotri*) (USSR, Byelorusfilm/Mosfilm, dir. Elem Klimov, 1985)

Convoy (GB, Ealing, dir. Penrose Tennyson, 1940)

Cross of Iron (GB/West Germany, EMI/Rapid/Terra Filmkunst, dir. Sam Peckinpah, 1977)

Cruel Sea, The (GB, Ealing, dir. Charles Crichton, 1953)

Dam Busters, The (GB, Associated British, dir. Michael Anderson, 1955)

Deer Hunter, The (USA, Universal/EMI, dir. Michael Cimino, 1978)

Desert Fox, The (USA, Twentieth Century-Fox, dir. Henry Hathaway, 1951)

Desert Victory (GB, Army Film and Photographic Unit, dir. Roy Boulting, 1943)

The Devil's General (*Des Teufels General*) (GFR, Ryal, dir. Helmut Käutner, 1955)

Dirty Dozen, The (USA, M-G-M, dir. Robert Aldrich, 1967)

Dunkirk (GB, M-G-M/Ealing, dir. Leslie Norman, 1958)

Eagle Has Landed, The (GB, ITC/Associated General, dir. John Sturges, 1976)

Europa Europa (France/Germany, Les Films du Losange/CCC Filmkunst/Perspektywa, dir. Agnieszka Holland, 1991)

First of the Few, The (GB, British Aviation Pictures, dir. Leslie Howard, 1942)

Five Cartridges (*Fünf Patronen-Hülsen*) (GDR, DEFA, dir. Frank Beyer, 1960)

Forever England (GB, Gaumont British, dir. Walter Forde, 1935)

Four Feathers, The (GB, London Films, dir. Zoltan Korda, 1939)

Full Metal Jacket (USA/GB, Warner Bros., dir. Stanley Kubrick, 1987)

Gallipoli (Australia, Associated, dir. Peter Weir, 1981)

Gardens of Stone (USA, Tristar, dir. Francis Ford Coppola, 1987)

Generation, A (*Pokolenie*) (Poland, Film Polski, dir. Andrzej Wajda, 1954)

Go Tell the Spartans (USA, Spartan, dir. Ted Post, 1978)

Grande Illusion, La (France, Réalisations d'Art Cinématographique, dir. Jean Renoir, 1937)

Great Escape, The (USA, United Artists/Mirish, dir. John Sturges, 1963)

Green Berets, The (USA, Warner Bros./Batjac, dir. John Wayne, 1968)

Gunga Din (USA, RKO Radio, dir. George Stevens, 1939)

Guns of Loos, The (GB, Stoll, dir. Sinclair Hill, 1928)

Guns of Navarone, The (GB, Columbia, dir. J. Lee Thompson, 1961)

Hamburger Hill (USA, Paramount, dir. John Irvin, 1987)

Hannibal Brooks (GB, United Artists/Scimitar, dir. Michael Winner, 1969)

Henry V (GB, Rank/Two Cities, dir. Laurence Olivier, 1944)

Heroes of Telemark, The (GB, Rank, dir. Anthony Mann, 1965)

How I Won the War (GB, United Artists/Petersham, dir. Richard Lester, 1967)

I Was Nineteen (*Ich war neunzehn*) (GDR, DEFA, dir. Konrad Wolf, 1968)

Ice Cold in Alex (GB, Associated British, dir. J. Lee Thompson, 1958)

In Which We Serve (GB, Two Cities, dir. Noëël Coward and David Lean, 1942)

Independence Day (USA, Twentieth Century-Fox, dir. Roland Emmerich, 1996)

Is Paris Burning? (*Paris brûle-t-il?*) (France/USA, Paramount/Transcontinental, dir. René Clément, 1965)

Ivan's Childhood (USSR, Mosfilm, dir. Andrei Tarkovskii, 1962)

J'accuse (*I Accuse*) (France, Pathé, dir. Abel Gance, 1919)

Jackboot Mutiny, The (*Es geschah am 20. Juli*) (FRG, Cine International, dir. G. W. Pabst, 1955)

Journey's End (GB, Gainsborough/Welsh-Pearson, dir. James Whale, 1930)

Kanal (Poland, Film Polski, dir. Andrzej Wajda, 1956)

Kelly's Heroes (USA/Yugoslavia, M-G-M. dir. Brian G. Hutton, 1970)

King and Country (GB, Warner-Pathé/BHE Productions, dir. Joseph Losey, 1964)

Lacombe, Lucien (France, Rank/NEF/UPF/Vides/Hallelujah Films, dir. Louis Malle, 1974)

Landscape After Battle (*Krajobraz Po Bitwe*) (Poland, Film Polski, dir. Andrzej Wajda, 1970)

Life is Beautiful (*La vita è bella*) (Italy, dir. Roberto Benigni, 1998)

Long Day's Dying, The (GB, Paramount, dir Peter Collinson, 1968)

Longest Day, The (USA, Twentieth Century-Fox, dir. Andrew Morton, Ken Annakin, Bernhard Wicki, 1962)

Lord of the Rings: The Return of the King, The (USA/New Zealand, New Line Cinema, dir. Peter Jackson, 2003)

Lord of the Rings: The Two Towers, The (USA/New Zealand, New Line Cinema, dir. Peter Jackson, 2002)

Master and Commander: The Far Side of the World (USA, Twentieth Century-Fox/Universal Miramax, dir. Peter Weir, 2003)

Memphis Belle, The (USA, War Activities Commission, dir. William Wyler, 1944)

Memphis Belle (USA/GB, Warner Bros./Enigma, dir. Michael Caton Jones, 1990)

Missing in Action (USA, Cannon, dir. Joseph Zito, 1984)

Mosquito Squadron (GB, United Artists, dir. Boris Sagal, 1968)

Next of Kin, The (GB, Ealing, dir. Thorold Dickinson, 1942)

Night Porter, The (Italy, Lotar Films, dir. Liliana Cavani, 1973)

Nine Men (GB, Ealing, dir. Harry Watt, 1943)

O.H.M.S. (GB, Gaumont British, dir. Raoul Walsh, 1936)

Objective: Burma! (USA, Warner Bros., dir. Raoul Walsh, 1945)

Oh! What A Lovely War (GB, Paramount, dir. Richard Attenborough, 1969)

Operation Crossbow (GB, M-G-M, dir. Michael Anderson, 1965)

Other Side, The (*Die Andere Seite*) (Germany, Candofilm, dir. Heinz Paul, 1931)

Passenger (*Pasazerka*) (Poland, Film Polski, dir. Andrzej Munk, 1963)

Paths of Glory (USA, United Artists/Bryna, dir. Stanley Kubrick, 1957)

Patton (USA, Twentieth Century-Fox, dir. Franklin Schaffner, 1970)

Platoon (USA, Orion/Hemdale, dir. Oliver Stone, 1986)

Play Dirty (GB, United Artists/Lowndes, dir. André de Toth, 1969)

Punishment Battalion 999 (*Strafbataillon 999*) (FRG, Taurisfilm, dir. Harald Philipp, 1959)

Quax the Test Pilot (*Quax, der Bruchpilot*) (Germany, Terra-Filmkunst, dir. Kurt Hoffmann, 1941)

Raid on Rommel (USA, Universal, dir. Henry Hathaway, 1971)

Rambo: First Blood Part II (USA, Carolco, dir. George Pan Cosmatos, 1985)

Reach for the Sky (GB, Rank, dir. Lewis Gilbert, 1956)

Red Bad of Courage, The (USA, M-G-M, dir. John Huston, 1951)

Sailor of the King (*Single-Handed*) (GB, Twentieth Century-Fox, dir. Roy Boulting, 1953)

Sands of Iwo Jima (USA, Republic, dir. Allan Dwan, 1949)

Saving Private Ryan (USA, DreamWorks, dir. Steven Spielberg, 1998)

Schindler's List (USA, Universal/Amblin, dir. Steven Spielberg, 1993)

Sea Wolves, The (GB, Richmond, dir. Andrew V. McLaglen, 1980)

Sergeant York (USA, Warner Bros., dir. Howard Hawks, 1941)

Seven Beauties (*Pasqualino settebellezze*) (Italy, Medua, dir. Lina Wertmüüller, 1975)

Ships With Wings (GB, Ealing, dir. Sergei Nolbandov, 1941)

633 Squadron (GB, United Artists/Mirisch, dir. Walter E. Grauman, 1964)

Stalingrad (*Dogs, Do You Want To Live Forever?/Hunde, wollt ihr ewig leben?*) (GFR, Taurusfilm, dir. Frank Wisbar, 1958)

Stalingrad (Germany, Royal/Bavaria/BA/Perathon, dir. Joseph Vilsmaier, 1991)

Star of Africa, The (*Der Stern von Afrika*) (FRG, Taurusfilm, dir. Alfred Weidenmann, 1957)

Star Wars (USA, Twentieth Century-Fox, dir. George Lucas, 1977)

Starship Troopers (USA, Touchstone/Tristar, dir. Paul Verhoeven, 1997)

Story of GI Joe, The (USA, United Artists, dir. William A. Wellman, 1945)

Sullivans, The (USA, Twentieth Century-Fox, dir. Lloyd Bacon, 1944)

Target for Tonight (GB, Crown Film Unit, dir. Harry Watt, 1941)

Tell England (GB, British Instructional, dir. Anthony Asquith, 1931)

They Were Expendable (USA, M-G-M, dir. John Ford, 1944)

They Who Dare (GB, British Lion, dir. Lewis Milestone, 1953)

Three Kings (USA, Warner Bros./Village Roadshow, dir. David O. Russell, 1999)

Too Late the Hero (USA, United Artists/Aldrich Associates, dir. Robert Aldrich,
   1970)

Top Gun (USA, Paramount, dir. Tony Scott, 1986)

Twelve O'Clock High (USA, Twentieth Century-Fox, dir. Henry King, 1949)

True Glory, The (GB/USA, Allied Film Services, dir. Carol Reed and Garson
   Kanin, 1945)

Victors, The (GB, Columbia, dir. Carl Foreman, 1963)

Walk in the Sun, A (USA, United Artists, dir. Lewis Milestone, 1945)

Way Ahead, The (GB, Two Cities, dir. Carol Reed, 1944)

We Dive at Dawn (GB, Gainsborough, dir. Anthony Asquith, 1943)

We Were Soldiers (USA, Paramount/Icon, dir. Randall Wallace, 2002)

Welcome to Sarajevo (GB, Channel 4/Miramax, dir. Michael Winterbottom, 1997)

Went the Day Well? (GB, Ealing, dir. Alberto Cavalcanti, 1942)

Western Approaches (GB, Crown Film Unit, dir. Pat Jackson, 1944)

Westfront 1918 (Germany, Nero-Film AG, dir. G. W. Pabst, 1930)

Where Eagles Dare (GB, M-G-M, dir. Brian G. Hutton, 1969)

Windtalkers (USA, M-G-M, dir. John Woo, 2004)

Wings (USA, Paramount, dir. William Wellman, 1927)

Winter War, The (*Talvisota*) (Finland, Nordisk, dir. Pekka Prikka, 1990)

Zulu (GB, Paramount/Joseph E. Levine, dir. Cy Endfield, 1964)

acknowledgements

My thanks are due to Vivian Constantinopoulos at Reaktion for commissioning this book for the *Locations* series and for her enthusiastic support of the project from its inception through to publication. Some of the arguments put forward in the pages that follow have taken shape through conversation with Jeremy Black, Robert Murphy, Michael Paris, Jeffrey Richards and Pierre Sorlin – none of whom bears any responsibility for my flights of interpretational fancy. My ideas on war and film have also taken shape through contributing to the Open University courses AA312 *Total War and Social Change: Europe, 1914–1955* and AA300 *Europe: Culture and Identities in a Contested Continent*: I am grateful to Tony Aldgate and Clive Emsley for their erudition and collegiality. My thanks to Michael Coyne for providing a copy of *The Victors* and to Sally Dux for *Oh! What a Lovely War*. Finally, I should record my thanks to my parents for letting me stay up to watch *Where Eagles Dare* on television when I was eight.

This book is dedicated to the memory of the late Professor Arthur Marwick (1936–2006), a respected colleague and a good friend. 'Life is always better after lunch.'

photo acknowledgements

Arca-Film/Ariston-Film: p. 145; Army Film Unit Production Company: pp. 26, 27; Army Film Unit Production Company/Royal Air Force Film Production Unit: p. 55; Associated British Picture Corporation: pp. 69, 230 (top), 231 (top), 233 (left); Associated General Films/ITC Entertainment: p. 226; Bavaria Atelier GmbH/Radiant-Film: p. 150; British Topical Committee for War Films: pp. 41, 42, 44; Carolco Pictures, Inc./Anabasis: pp. 172, 173, 179, 181; CCC Filmkunst/Zeyn: p. 147; Channel Four Television Corporation: pp. 100, 101; DreamWorks/Paramount Pictures/Amblin Entertainment: pp. 18, 19, 21, 23; Film Polski: pp. 74, 143; Harris-Kubrick Pictures Corporation: p. 133 (top); Hemdale Film Corporation/Orion Pictures Corporation: p. 163; London Film Productions: p. 191; Lucasfilm/Twentieth Century Fox Film Corporation: pp. 230 (middle), 231 (middle), 233 (right); Mayflower Pictures Corporation: p. 212; Metro-Goldwyn-Mayer, Inc./Kenneth Hyman Production: p. 219; Metro-Goldwyn-Mayer, Inc./Warriors Company: p. 223; Metro-Goldwyn-Mayer, Inc./Winkast Film Productions: pp. 204, 206; Mirisch Company/Alpha Company: p. 201; Mosfilm Studios: pp. 77, 78, 105, 107, 114, 115; Neue Emelka/Producciones Cinematograficas Ariel: p. 194; Omni Zoetrope: pp. 89, 164, 165; Open Road Films: pp. 214, 215; Paramount Pictures Corporation/Accord Productions, Ltd: p. 135; Perathon Film- und Fernsehproduktions/Bavaria-Film/Geiselgasteig-Film Produktionsgesellschaft /B.A.- Film Produktion: p. 151; Pinnacle Productions: p. 195; Réalisations d'Art Cinématographique: p. 121; Spitfire Productions: p. 82; Twentieth Century Fox Film Corporation/Universal Studios /Miramax Film Corp.: p. 241; Two Cities Films: pp. 85, 86; United Artists: p. 81; Universal Pictures: pp. 48, 49, 124, 127; Universal Pictures/Amblin Entertainment: p. 159; Warner Bros: p. 210; Warner Bros/Natant Films: p. 169; Zespól Filmowy 'Kadr': pp. 75, 76.

index